Chicago Crime Stories
Rich Gone Wrong

Bryan W. Alaspa

Schiffer Publishing Ltd

4880 Lower Valley Road Atglen, Pennsylvania 19310

Please visit our web site catalog at www.schifferbooks.com

We are always looking for people to write books on new and related subjects. If you have an idea for a book, please contact us at the above address.

This book may be purchased from the publisher.
Include $5.00 for shipping.
Please try your bookstore first.
You may write for a free catalog.

In Europe, Schiffer books are distributed by:
Bushwood Books
6 Marksbury Ave.
Kew Gardens
Surrey TW9 4JF
England
Phone: 44 (0)208 392-8585
Fax: 44 (0)208 392-9876
E-mail: Info@bushwoodbooks.co.uk

Website: www.bushwoodbooks.co.uk
Free postage in the UK. Europe: air mail at cost.
Try your bookstore first.

6 Marksbury Ave.
Kew Gardens
Surrey TW9 4JF England
Phone: 44 (0) 20 8392-8585; Fax: 44 (0) 20 8392-9876
E-mail: info@bushwoodbooks.co.uk
Website: www.bushwoodbooks.co.uk
Free postage in the U.K., Europe; air mail at cost.

Cover image: Crime©Gonzalo Medina. Image from BigStockPhoto.com
Inside images: Chicago Night Glow©Peter Tambroni. Image from BigStockPhoto.com
Tablets©Sergey Galushko.Image from BigStockPhoto.com
Courtroom Scene©Nikolay Mamluke. Image from BigStockPhoto.com
Brown and White Spanish Horses in a Green Field©Nick Stubbs. Image from BigStockPhoto.com

Printed in China
Schiffer Books are available at special discounts for bulk purchases for sales promotions or premiums.
Special editions, including personalized covers, corporate imprints, and excerpts can be created in large quantities for special needs. For more information contact the publisher:

Published by Schiffer Publishing Ltd.
4880 Lower Valley Road
Atglen, PA 19310
Phone: (610) 593-1777; Fax: (610) 593-2002
E-mail: Info@schifferbooks.com

Dedication

To Zoe, the apple of her uncle's eye.

Foreword
The Lawless City

The city of Chicago sits today next to Lake Michigan as grand and shining as any worldly city. Its buildings stretch upwards toward the sky like man-made fingers. The streets are paved and lined with hundreds, thousands, perhaps millions, of cars—all belching their smoke and noise into the air. By anyone's standards it is a modern, civilized place.

However, Chicago has a very long history. It was a place known by the Native Americans who lived in and traveled through Illinois. The very name of Chicago is derived from the French spelling and pronunciation of a Native American word that meant "smelly onions" due to the huge onion field that was once located where Chicago is now.

Chicago's rise from a field of onions, to a trading post, to a fort, to a town, to a city, is truly one of speed and rapidity. At one time, the city of Chicago was the fastest-growing city in the country. It was also, at one time, about as far west as you could go. It progressed from a simple town into a city of over a hundred thousand people faster than any other city. Then came the famous World's Fair, the Ferris Wheel, and the skyscrapers.

At the same time, the history of Chicago is marred repeatedly by violence—and violence of the most shocking variety. It cannot be forgotten that Ford Dearborn, which was located in what is now downtown Chicago, was the scene of a famous battle and subsequent massacre. It cannot be forgotten that, while the city of white shimmered before the world during the World's Fair, a man named H. H. Holmes had constructed a house of horror meant for killing people not very far away.

There has seldom been a city where progress and violence has been linked so thoroughly. Chicago was the home of Al Capone, after all, and the scene of the St. Valentine's Day Massacre. It is the place where a pockmarked drifter named Richard Speck decided to murder eight student nurses in the course of a single night. It is also the place where a respected businessman and birthday party clown named John Wayne Gacy murdered thirty-five young men and buried many of them in the crawl-space of his house in the suburbs.

So, throughout the history of Chicago there have been heroes and there have been villains. For some reason, however, the Chicago villains seem to be a different breed. Even the mob thought of the Chicago gangsters as barbarians. It wasn't enough for Gacy to just be a serial killer; he had to hold the record, for a time, as America's most prolific (sadly a record that has since been eclipsed).

Chicago is not a place lined with celebrities. Sure, there have been and continue to be many rich and famous people who call Chicago home. These are not your typical movie stars, however. Chicago has always been known as a blue collar, working-class town and their rich and famous tend to be the type who have clawed and climbed their way to the top.

Just like in other places, those rich and famous have sometimes been murdered. In Chicago, however, there have been many cases when those rich and famous have been the ones committing the murders. Let's not forget that Al Capone, while a gangster, was also a vastly wealthy gangster and a staunch community leader.

So, now it is time to take a tour through some of the most notorious crimes that have dotted the history of this great and grand city. Along the way you will meet one of the world's most notorious and blood-thirsty villains that you are ever likely to meet. He is a man who deserves to stand in the halls of the notorious of this city along with Capone and Gacy and Speck. You will also meet the cast of characters who have been involved in some of the biggest crimes, many of them still unsolved, and cases that you have probably never heard about.

Chicago is sometimes referred to as the "City of Big Shoulders." You will see that it is also the "City of Big Crimes."

Contents

Part One
Silas

An Introduction
Silas, the Stone-Cold Killer

The idea of the wealthy man who is also heartless and villainous is one almost as old as fiction itself. Every character from Ebenezer Scrooge to J.R. Ewing could fall into that category. In real life, many would argue, these men are not really that ruthless. Real men who make their money through hard work don't have time to plot the deaths of others.

Well, it turns out that isn't quite the case.

By all accounts, the man named Silas Jayne was an intimidating man. During his trial, he was reported to stare fixedly at the jury. His eyes would bore into them, causing many of them to feel uncomfortable.

Silas was a man who made his money in horses. He bred, sold and managed show horses. He set up shop not far from Chicago, and quickly gained a reputation as well as a small fortune. His methods of acquiring that fortune, however, have now become the stuff of legend.

According to his family, Silas began to show signs of being a sociopath at a very young age. The tale goes that, at about the age of six, he was bitten by a goose that was living on his family's farm. Silas decided that revenge was required. However, Silas felt that true revenge could only be exacted by killing the goose, and the entire flock the goose belonged to, with an axe. So, later, when he came into the home covered in blood and feathers, he had to explain to his family why he had slaughtered so many birds.

It is also a cliché in fiction of the villain that will not just kill you, but kill your entire family. It seems that Silas Jayne was really that kind of villain.

While the mob was running Chicago, Silas was setting up

his own kind of mob in the suburbs. No one wanted to refuse anything that Silas wanted. If he wanted a horse you owned, you had better just sell it to him. If you didn't, your barns might burn down, your remaining horses might be killed, or a bomb might destroy large portions of your ranch. If that still didn't work, bullets could end up smashing through your living room window, and you had better have someone else start your car for you. Rumor has it that even the mob was frightened of Silas Jayne and wanted to leave him alone in his suburban empire.

Silas was not afraid to use his ruthless nature against his own family. When his brother George broke away from Silas and set up his own breeding facility, he became competition for Silas. When George won a major competition and then stole a rider from Silas, there were threats thrown. Thus began a feud between the two brothers that would leave bloodshed of epic proportions on both sides.

Silas surrounded himself with scum. He put people who could do the dirty work for him all around him. These were men with peculiar desires and murderous tendencies. They were loyal and willing to do Silas' work for him. He paid well and, well, he was also scary.

Silas once shot a man who was on his property with a machine gun. According to Silas, this man pulled a gun and fired at him. He then returned fire and hit the man as he attempted to climb a fence. Again, according to Silas, he reached into his arsenal and pulled out his carbine and gunned the man down on his front lawn. The police determined that it was self-defense.

The feud between his brother resulted in much collateral damage. It ultimately ended in the death of his brother, who was shot down in front of his family during his son's sixteenth birthday party. Silas had won the feud, but it did, finally, cost him his freedom.

Silas Jayne would spend seven years in prison. When he came

out, he continued to protest his innocence. He ultimately died in the 80s of leukemia, in his bed, in his sleep. It was a death so peaceful that many who knew him were shocked.

Once he was dead, those who knew of his monstrous past felt it safe to come forward. This is why Silas Jayne deserves to be ranked among Chicago's most notorious monsters. His name comes up in not just one, but three of Chicago's most famous, brutal, and most infamous murders.

Silas Jayne was rich. He was relatively famous. Most importantly, he was a stone-cold killer.

Chapter One
The Schuessler-Peterson Murders

The year was 1955 and the month was October. The city of Chicago was like most cities at that time and experiencing the economic boom that was going along with the winning of World War II. In the northwest suburbs of Chicago, many young married couples and their families had begun to set up homes and set about living the lives they had dreamed of. The Schuessler and Peterson families were among those.

It was a typical Sunday afternoon that October when John and Anton Schuessler and their friend Bobby Peterson asked for permission to take public transportation downtown to see a matinee movie. Both sets of parents gave permission and Bobby's mother picked the film they were to see. They were given money and with the princely sum of $4 between them, the boys set off for the city and the movies.

Of course, back then, such things were common. Although the boys were young, they had always proven to be dependable. Neither set of parents ever expressed any reservations about them heading downtown or being left on their own.

The boys made it to the movies and saw a matinee. At 6 p.m. they were seen in the lobby of a building known as the Garland Building which was at 111 North Wabash. No one was ever sure what they were doing there. The only thing that the building had in common with the boys was that Bobby Peterson's eye doctor had an office in there. Regardless of the reason they were there, they did not stay long.

At 7:45 p.m., the three boys were seen entering the Monte

Cristo Bowling Alley located on West Montrose. There was a restaurant in the bowling alley and it was a popular hang out for kids in the area. The man who ran the place saw the three young men there and noticed that there was a man who looked to be about "fifty-ish" taking an "abnormal interest" in the three boys. Since the place was busy, he did not see if this man ever actually spoke to the three young men or not.

Eventually, the three young boys left the Monte Cristo and walked down Montrose to another bowling alley. The time was about 9:05 p.m. and the three boys were out of money. Back home, their parents were starting to worry.

Exactly what happened between 9:05 p.m. on that day and the day (two days later) when their bodies were found, would not be known for decades. It would, according to many, shatter whatever innocence Chicago and its suburbs may have had. It would also shock the community so deeply that mothers would forever fret about talking to strangers. The days of parents letting their young children travel downtown alone were pretty much over.

It was a salesman who first found the bodies. They were in a ditch maybe 100 feet from the Des Plaines River. The salesman had pulled over by the side of the road to eat some lunch. At first, when he saw the pale skin and the naked bodies, he thought they were store mannequins. Then he paused and looked a bit closer. Moments later he was scrambling for a phone and calling the police.

Chicago city police, along with several suburban police agencies, all responded to the scene. All of them immediately began trampling the area and destroying evidence by sheer lack of communication. A search of the nearby woods was conducted, but with so many men—and none of them coordinated or communicating—the search was completely fruitless. No trace of the boys' clothing was ever found.

The investigation was botched almost from the beginning. Even before police arrived, an aide to the coroner moved the bodies to help out a photographer from a local newspaper. Reporters were there before the police, stepping all over crucial areas where forensic evidence may have lain.

Bobby Peterson had been beaten about the head. He had then been strangled with a rope or perhaps a necktie. The other two boys were killed by "asphyxiation by suffocation" according to Coroner Walter McCarron. McCarron also stated that he thought the boys had been dead about thirty-six hours before they were found.

The boys' eyes had been taped shut using adhesive tape. Beyond that, it seemed that the killer or killers had gone to great lengths to cover up and hide any evidence. No fingerprints were found. Nothing was discovered in or around the bodies. No one stepped forward as a witness.

The father of Anton Schuessler stated, "When you get the point that children cannot go to the movies in the afternoon and get home safely, something is wrong with this country."

Panic gripped the entire city. Parents began locking their children up at night. Children were not allowed to go anywhere unaccompanied. Several of the police agencies made public statements that they had never seen a crime as horrific as this one.

The boys were buried in St. Joseph Cemetery. An honor guard of Boy Scouts carried the three coffins from St. Tarcissus Roman Catholic Church to the hearse. The church was filled with over 1,200 mourners on the day of the funeral. Meanwhile the police were coming up empty on every front.

Once the case was shifted to a task force, it was given to investigators who had never actually been to the crime scene. The task force set about attempting to track down every lead. They ended up interviewing thousands of people and amassed over 6,000 pages of reports in the hopes of tracking down the killer or killers. They came up with very little.

There is no statute of limitations for murder. As such, the case remained open. Investigators felt, early on, that the Idle Hour Stables, owned by a man named Silas Jayne, was the likely spot for the crime. Residents who lived near the stables reported to police that they had heard children screaming near them on the night the three boys were last seen alive. Others reported hearing the sound of a car tearing off into the night.

At that time, Silas Jayne was not well known to police. He had a general reputation of being a tough guy and a bit of a brute, but the true nature of his criminal mind was not know by police. In fact, he was even respected by those in the neighborhood and within the horse breeding industry at that point.

The police needed only to look at a map to see why the Idle Hours Stable might be the location for the murders. It was not terribly far from the place where the boys had been found. It was just isolated enough to provide the seclusion needed to commit such a crime. This, plus the testimony of the residents, raised suspicion amongst investigators. There was just one problem. None of them had any hard evidence.

A team of detectives visited the Idle Hour Stables just ten days after the bodies of the young boys were found. They came back to the station without a suspect. No one at the stables knew anything and no one had heard anything. They had no statements from anyone that would warrant further investigations. There was nothing that could definitively point to a suspect. At the same time, the investigators had only spoken to an elderly couple who lived on the grounds and four stable hands. They neglected to speak to Silas.

One of the men they spoke to was a man named Kenneth Hansen. Hansen was reportedly a worker at the Idle Hands

Stable. He was also very close to Silas. He was so close to him that he often referred to him as "Uncle Si." However, there was evidently nothing suspicious enough about Hansen to justify bringing him in for further questioning or arresting him.

Years later, long after Silas Jayne was dead, the investigators who had inherited the case, would look back on those investigations and wonder why leads were not followed up. Of course, it was also thought that Silas Jayne had started to use his money and influence to essentially "buy off" investigators and police officials. In fact, just a few years after the murders, Silas would practically own several small suburban police forces.

The police went back to the stables on December 5. Again, they came back empty-handed. The case was growing cold.

Years passed. The files and the pages of reports were passed from one generation of cops to the next. No new leads were developed. Investigators were suspicious of Hansen and they had their suspicions about the involvement of Silas Jayne, but no new evidence came about.

Meanwhile, Silas Jayne was continuing his reign of terror within the show-horse breeding community. He was engaged in shady deals, bilking people out of money and then threatening those who dared try to take him to task. He threw his weight around, bought those he could, and threatened and harmed those he couldn't. He bought silence and he kept that silence through fear.

Within the same year as the death of the three boys, two young sisters were also found dead by the side of the road. It happened barely a year after the three boys. Again, the city of Chicago was thrown into a panic. The bodies were once again found in the suburbs and on the side of the road. Once again, the name of Silas Jayne was mentioned, but, once again, the investigation went nowhere.

Meanwhile, the Schuessler-Peterson murders were not forgotten. It remained one of the most brutal murder cases in the city of Chicago. It also remained one of the most notorious unsolved murder cases in the city's history.

There were many mysteries about what happened that night. No one could be sure why the boys were spotted at the Garland building the night of their disappearance. What could they have been doing there?

Many, many years later, one former police detective floated a theory. The detective, John Sarnowski, suggested that maybe the boys were there to meet a young man named John Wayne Gacy. Apparently, the lobby of the Garland building was a known meeting place for gay men and gay prostitutes. Of course, this is just a theory and there is no proof. It is known that Gacy was living in the area at that time, but whether or not he was supposed to meet the boys can only be surmised.

As the case remained unsolved, Silas Jayne began a feud with his brother. He killed a man on his front lawn. A bomb attached to his brother's car killed an innocent bystander. Finally, the people Silas hired to kill his brother, George, came forward and began to testify against him. Silas finally found himself in jail.

The problem was that Silas could still control his empire from behind bars, just like any thug or mobster. He continued to mastermind shady deals and became involved, many say, in another notorious murder. This time he may have been behind the disappearance of candy heiress Helen Brach.

Silas spent seven years in prison. He came out just before the 1980s and just before he turned 80. He declared his innocence. Then he contracted leukemia, at the same time federal agents gathered around him on both the Brach case and other cases involving federal offenses a mile long. Silas managed to outsmart them all by dying in his bed of leukemia.

It seems as though the world was just waiting for that to finally happen. Once Silas was gone, people began to step forward and talk about the life he had lead. While many knew that he was involved in the death of his own brother, none fully realized the extent to which his evil had crept.

From nowhere, a man who was in government protection and looking for further benefits decided to float some information he had found. He stated that he knew who had murdered the two boys, and who had helped that man cover it up. The man's name was William Wemette and the person he fingered was Kenneth Hansen, the man who had worked at Silas Jayne's stables, had been questioned when the bodies had been found, and never convicted because there had been no evidence.

Hansen was arrested and began denying everything, but with the name, the evidence began to come tumbling down. The story finally, years later, was ready to come out.

The investigators were able to find evidence showing that Hansen had run into the boys while they were in the city. He lured them into his car with the promise of showing them some prize horses back in the stables where he worked. For whatever reason, the boys climbed into the car. Hansen drove them to Jayne's stables and he began to have sex with one or perhaps two of the boys. The remaining boy saw what was happening and threatened to scream, run away, or to get the authorities. Hansen grabbed the boy and killed him to silence him. He then turned to the remaining two boys and killed them, too.

No sooner had the act been completed when Silas Jayne walked into the stable and found Hansen and the three bodies. Reportedly, Jayne flew into a rage. He accused Hansen of attempting to get him into trouble and then he agreed to help Hansen cover everything up.

Silas helped Hansen carry the bodies into a car and put

them in the trunk. They then set about burning the stables to the ground so little remained of the crime scene but dust. The two men then drove off into the night and crudely dumped the naked bodies on the side of the road.

It was 1995 when Hansen was arrested and came to trial. Hansen denied he ever worked for Jayne during the time when the boys disappeared. He denied ever seeing the boys or having anything to do with their deaths. It didn't matter. Finally, so many years after he had helped put terror into the hearts of the Chicago area and children everywhere, Hansen was convicted and sentenced to 300 years in prison. The jury took only two hours to convict him.

During the trial, other victims of Hansen's depravity and appetites came forward. Victim after victim testified of his sexual tendencies and his assaults on them. He had been abusing young boys for decades, and had several times threatened to do to them what he had done "to the Peterson boy" in order to keep them silent.

The souls of the young boys could now rest in peace. One of the most horrific and notorious crimes in Chicago history was now solved. As for Silas Jayne, however, the truth of what he had done throughout his life was only just coming out. He had more crimes under his belt.

Chapter Two
The Candy Heiress

Chicago is actually one of the biggest candy cities in the world. It may not be the first thing that jumps to your mind when you think of the city, but it is a place where candy is made. The M&M's/Mars people have a large factory located in Chicago. Blommers is the name of a chocolate manufacturer located near downtown and often filling the area with the smell of chocolate. At one time the famous Marshall Field store in downtown housed a small candy factory that made Frango Mints. Every year, a huge candy convention is held in Chicago. There are more famous names associated with candy and the City of Broad Shoulders.

If you have ever walked into a store and seen the hard candies and caramels in bins, wrapped in clear paper, with the word "BRACH" written across the wrapper, then you are familiar with the Brach candy dynasty. What you may not know is that the Brach family was from the Chicago area. More than likely, you didn't know that the Brach family was involved in one of the most notorious murders in the city's history.

Helen Vorhees Brach lived a quiet life in the northern suburbs of the city of Chicago. She lived in a huge house on a huge plot of land with her housekeepers and butlers and servants. She also had an intense love of horses and kept many of them on her acres and acres of land. She was also, by most accounts, alone, which made her a perfect target for a man associated with Silas Jayne.

By all accounts, Helen's life was one of solitude and loneliness. She was not a rich brat likely to be spotted out on the town during her younger years. She was quiet and kept to herself. The only thing that really made her famous was being an heiress to a huge family fortune and for having the name "Brach" associated with her.

It was Frank Brach who first found Helen and fell in love. Frank was the man who had turned the Brach candy company into a multi-million dollar corporation. He was also a man who loved visiting the Palm Beach County Club to spend his winters there. He was married when he first set eyes on a coat-check girl who worked there.

It wasn't long before Frank and Helen were dating, despite their age difference. It also wasn't long before he proposed and Helen accepted. The two were married and had a happy life together.

Helen was generous with her family, lavishing gifts upon her brothers, parents, and siblings. It was a bad habit to start, as it turned out. Before too long, her family came to rely on the money she would pour upon them.

Frank died at the age of 79 in 1970, while Helen was 58, and suddenly Helen was alone. Helen loved animals and she began to spend huge amounts of money on animal causes. At the same time, she also loved to wear fur. In addition to loving horses and keeping them on the huge parcels of land she owned, she also had dogs and other animals. She was considered eccentric because she was very into spiritualism and believed in automatic writing, the supposed belief that a spirit can take over a living person's body and give them messages through writing they are not aware they are doing. Finally, Helen was also a voracious and dedicated journal-keeper.

Richard Bailey was part of the notorious "Jayne Gang" as they were known in parts of Chicago. When it came to buying horses, they were the guys you went to. Of course, by the time Helen Brach disappeared, Silas Jayne was attracting the criminal element like moths to a flame. So, the guys you had to go to in order to buy a horse were also the likely guys who would scam you out of your money.

The scams that this group ran were relatively simple. They would attract a wealthy customer, most likely a woman such as Helen Brach. They would tell this "mark" that investing in horses was a lucrative proposition, or perhaps the person already had an interest in buying a horse. One of the gang would get friendly with this person and would then advise that they had a horse that should be purchased. Of course, it would turn out that the horse they were trying to sell the person was not nearly as valuable as stated.

The Jayne gang also had vets in their pocket who would certify a horse as being worth much more than it actually was. The mark would show up, agree to buy the horse, and often the agreement was to split the cost with another member of the gang, and once the mark had left, the check of the gang member would be torn up and the mark's check split between the rest of the gang.

With Richard Bailey, there was an additional element. Bailey was particularly adept at finding wealthy, older, lonely, rich women. He would convince them he was in love with them. He would wine and dine them and get them to fall in love with him. Then he would scam the money from them, split the earnings with the rest of the Jayne Gang, and move on to the next unsuspecting lady. Suddenly ol' Richard wouldn't return their phone calls or call on them anymore.

By the time Helen Brach ran into Richard Bailey, he was running the Bailey Stables and Country Club Stables. He would often run ads in the various publications under the Personals section. This was how he found the widows or divorced rich women upon who he preyed. He would make the high point of his courtship a visit to his stables and to his horses. Then he would take them to the finest restaurants and start sending flowers and expensive gifts. If he found out that the woman he was seeing was not as wealthy as he thought, he would quickly call everything off. If it turned out the woman was wealthier than he first thought, he would lure the woman to bed and even go so far as to propose marriage— even though Bailey himself was already married.

Silas Jayne himself was having problems during the 70s. He had finally found out that he was not as untouchable as he thought he was. Of course, murdering your own brother drew the kind of attention someone like Silas didn't want.

Although Silas had successfully scared and bullied away most of the witnesses to his crimes, he had finally run across the one man who wouldn't back down. So, Silas was in prison when Bailey and Brach ran into each other. Of course, as mentioned before and like all good crime lords, Silas managed to maintain his empire even from behind the walls of his cell.

Bailey had learned well at the feet of his mentor, Silas Jayne. He had a couple of scams he would work with the women who would fall in love with him. One scam involved telling the woman that his money was completely tied up but that he had discovered a horse that would make a tremendous investment for both of them. The two of them would then use the horse for collateral and Bailey would secure a temporary loan from his intended victim which he claimed he would use to buy the horse. He would then not repay the loan to the victim and the victim became responsible for boarding and care for the horse. Of course, Bailey's horse would be provided by a co-conspirator so they could now charge the victim for all kinds of strange charges and even take the horse back (to be used in another scam) when the victim couldn't pay the bills anymore.

The other scam he had was described above. He would get a co-conspirator to agree on a price for an over-valued horse. Then he would convince his victim to pay for half of the cost of the horse and he would write out a check for the other half. Once the victim left, his check would be torn up and the remaining money split.

The third scam involved convincing his victim to purchase an over-valued horse which did not suit her expected needs. When the victim would complain that the horse did not work well, run well, or breed well, he would suggest trading the horse for another more-expensive horse.

Helen Brach was nearly tailor-made as a victim for Bailey and the Jayne Gang. She was rich. She was well known for being alone. Finally, she loved horses. For a man like Richard Bailey, there couldn't have been a better mark. It was as if all of the scams he had run and helped run for Silas Jayne and his cronies were leading up to his fateful meeting with Helen Brach.

Bailey met Helen in 1973. He had been running his scams for a long time before then and had never been caught. He had left a long trail of broken-hearted widows and wealthy women and taken much of their cash. Bailey was romantic and dashing and incredibly charming. Helen Brach, the quiet, lonely candy heiress, didn't really stand a chance. They entered into a relationship almost immediately. Bailey spent time earning her trust and convincing her he loved her before he got involved in his first scam with her. That happened in 1975.

Bailey told Brach that he knew of three horses that she should buy. Luckily, the horses were owned by Bailey's brother, Paul. This should have made the sale easy. Plus it would be a way for Brach to help out Bailey's brother. Paul sold Helen the horse for $98,000 and, completely unknown to Helen,

Richard Bailey was intimately involved in the sale. Also, the horses were completely worthless—valued at about $20,000. Bailey, in addition to this, had bought a group of very expensive brood mares.

Brach was still entranced by Bailey. In 1977, they were reported to have "danced the night away" on New Years Eve. They were spotted doing their dancing and partying and swooning in New York at the Waldorf-Astoria. Soon after, though, things in their relationship began to head south.

In the early months of 1977, Bailey tried to entice more money out of Brach by introducing a new scam. Bailey and his cohort arranged for a huge showing for Brach in the hopes that she might invest $150,000 for more horses. Brach showed up at the showing, but left before she had stayed an entire hour. At the same time, an appraiser had looked at the original three horses Bailey had convinced her to invest in and told her not to invest anymore money in them. Finally, Brach had visited her stables and seen the mares Bailey had purchased and was seen screaming to anyone and everyone manning her stables that she had been cheated and that she was going to head to the district attorney's office.

Meanwhile, pulling the strings, offering advice, and guiding those he had trained in these scams was Silas Jayne. He was still maintaining his innocence with his brother's death and murder. He received regular visitors, however, from the Jayne Gang. When he was eventually released, he was not poor and he was also being investigated by the FBI and other law-enforcement agencies for more scams and crimes. Exactly how much he was involved in the Brach disappearance is still unknown because Silas managed to outwit the law enforcement agencies by dying before charges could be brought against him for the Brach murder.

While Helen had loudly exclaimed that she would be visiting the District Attorney's office and bring charges against Bailey and anyone else she could think of, the gang turned to Silas for advice. The rumor has it that he told them that Helen Brach needed to disappear—and to disappear permanently. Rumor also has it, he even told them how they could go about making that happen.

Helen was scheduled to visit the Mayo Clinic and she had found a friend who knew someone at the State's Attorney's office and had set up a meeting with that person once she had returned. Helen Brach left the Mayo Clinic on February 17, 1977. She was never seen again and her body has never been found.

Helen was eventually reported missing by friends and family. Given that she was a Brach, the authorities turned much of their resources toward finding the missing woman. Right from the beginning there was a bad feeling about what had happened to Helen.

The investigators asked Helen's friends when they last saw her. According to her longtime handyman, John Matlick claimed that he took Helen to O'Hare Airport where she was, according to him, going to get on a plane for Florida. A quick check showed that Helen had never purchased a plane ticket for Florida, particularly not during the time frame Matlick was touting.

It wasn't long before the investigation went absolutely cold. The investigators could not find a body. They could not find any evidence one way or another whether Helen was alive or dead. There was no blood anywhere and no traces of human remains. It truly seemed as if Helen had vanished from the face of the planet.

The investigators found out about Bailey and they also quickly found out about his previous activities with other lonely but wealthy women. They also noticed that the handyman,

Matlick, was suddenly spending money like it was going out of style. When he was asked about his sudden wealth, Matlick stated he had gotten his money by selling some rare coins.

In June of 1979, Bailey was brought in for questioning. This was not a trial, but merely a deposition, where he sat in a room and answered questions from lawyers representing the Brach family and Helen's estate. Bailey took the Fifth Amendment and refused to answer questions about where Helen may be or when he last saw her.

Although federal agents were without a body, they were starting to piece together some bits and pieces. Some names began to pop up and they were names that rang alarm bells amongst law enforcement officials in and around Chicago. As you may have guessed, the one name that rang the loudest bells was that of Jayne.

Not only was Silas Jayne's name mentioned, but his nephew Frank Jayne, Jr. was also mentioned. Some further probing turned up evidence of the bait-and-switch schemes the Jayne clan had committed on others. At the same time, the butler and supposed friend of Brach, Jack Matlick, was still spending money. It was believed by the investigators that it might have been Matlick who drove Brach from her appointment at the Mayo Clinic into the hands of the people who killed her. Why did they kill her? Investigators felt that her threats were being taken seriously and she had to be kept quiet.

The Bureau of Alcohol Tobacco and Firearms was in charge of the federal investigation. They felt they knew who was involved, but they didn't have the evidence they needed to make an official arrest. The years ticked by and by 1984, Brach was officially declared dead. When that happened, her fortune was divided amongst the Helen Brach Foundation, her brother, and Jack Matlick. Once again, those investigating the murders bristled at the sight of Matlick spending money they knew he had gotten through criminal acts, but were helpless to do anything about it.

As was mentioned before, Silas Jayne outwitted everyone by dying not long after he was released from prison. Whatever he knew about masterminding or being involved in Brach's disappearance went with him. At the same time, just to add to the confusion, others began to step forward claiming to have information about Brach and where her body was located.

In January of 1988, a one-time inmate came forward and claimed to have helped bury Brach's body in Minnesota as a favor to Silas Jayne. Immediately, the federal investigators dispatched an army of investigators to search the areas where the informer claims to have taken the body. They turned up nothing.

In December of 1990, the badly decomposed body of a woman was found in a forest preserve in Cook County. Her body was dug up and taken to the Cook Count medical examiner's office. An autopsy was done while speculation ran rampant that the body of Helen Brach has been found. Cook County said that the body was not Brach's, but the federal investigators refused to cross the body off of their list.

In September of 1993, Jack Matlick's spending spree comes to an end at the behest of a judge. Cook County Judge Henry Budzinski tells Matlick that he has to repay $90,000 to Helen Brach's estate. That total includes $15,000 in bogus checks that were forged using Brach's bank account after she went missing. It also included $75,000 in cold, hard cash.

The investigators finally decided they had enough evidence to at least bring Bailey to trial. He was arrested in July of 1994. One of the key reasons charges were finally brought against Bailey was because of a man named Joe Plemmons, a former horse trainer and employee of the Jayne family.

Plemmons came forward to authorities and confirmed

that it was Silas Jayne, along with Frank Jayne, Jr., who had ordered the murder of Helen Brach. He also confirmed that Jack Matlick drove Brach from her doctor's appointment to the place where her killers were waiting. Brach had grown to trust Matlick and it was key to the entire plan that he be involved in the transportation. As such, Brach came willingly into the hands of the people who would end her life.

Plemmons stated that there were two people involved in the actual murder of the candy heiress. The first was former Skokie Police Sergeant Lee Reiter who did side work as a bodyguard for the Jayne family. He was also a trusted enforcer and was tapped to help out this time as well. Plemmons then named himself as the second hand involved in the actual murder. He then told the investigators what happened to Brach on her last moments on earth.

Matlick drove Brach to her home where Reiter was already waiting, having just been paid hundreds of thousands of dollars for his work. Upon entering her home, Reiter attacked Brach and beat her unconscious. According to Plemmons, the beating was particularly vicious because he'd seen her bruised and battered body after it had been wrapped in a blanket and stuffed into the trunk of a car prior to being driven to the Chicago suburb of Tinley Park where the Jayne family had a horse stable. This was when Plemmons was brought in.

The body moved and during the time it moved, someone thought they heard her moan. Plemmons himself said he thought she was already dead. Two other stable workers, Ken and Curt Hansen were also there and they both told Plemmons that they'd heard her moan. According to Plemmons, Curt Hansen pointed a loaded shotgun at him and then handed him a revolver. Plemmons fired two shots into the blanket and the body beneath.

Plemmons was then recruited as part of the disposal team.

He also claims that Frank Jayne, Jr. and both Hansen brothers were assigned the job of disposing of the body. Just to make things even more interesting, Plemmons claimed two members of the famous Spilotro mob family were also in attendance. It was the mobsters who supposedly provided the Jaynes with the actual method of destroying the body.

The disposal site was in nearby Northwest Indiana in a steel mill blast furnace. Plemmons told authorities that he and the Hansens tossed the body and blanket into the furnace while Jayne, Jr. stood by and watched.

All of those mentioned in Plemmon's statement have denied any involvement in Brach's disappearance. Matlick has never been charged with anything and still lives in Pennsylvania. Frank Jayne, Jr. was eventually brought up on charges of arson on an unrelated case and was sentenced to prison in Illinois. Reiter, the former police sergeant, claims he had nothing to do with Brach's vanishing and now lives in Mexico. Curt Hansen has since died and Ken Hansen is in prison for the Schuessler-Peterson murders.

Despite these denials, the authorities have claimed they feel the statement is the accurate description of the events around Brach's disappearance. Notwithstanding this, however, it is only one witness and there has never been any further evidence to link the men discussed in the statement to bring them up on charges. Plemmons was used, however, in a sentencing hearing against Bailey who, as of this date, is still the only person ever brought up on charges of any kind in connection with the vanishing and presumed murder of Helen Brach.

During the trial, the deeds of Richard Bailey were made public. Although his defense team tried every trick they knew to keep his past dealings with women out of the case, it was to no avail. The judge heard woman after woman and relative after relative testify against Bailey and explain how even before he had decided to participate in the death of Helen Brach, he had driven many women to the point of death with his attempts at romance and in milking them dry.

Richard Bailey was sentenced to life in prison and ordered to pay a fine of one million dollars. He sits in a federal prison to this day, still the only man convicted or imprisoned that had anything to do with the death of Helen Brach.

Also to this day, no trace of Helen's body have ever been found.

Chapter Three
The Brother

By all accounts, Silas Jayne was a man built for being ruthless and for being a bully. Jayne had a muscular build, and played up his cowboy image. He wore a cowboy hat, built up his body, had skin hardened from the sun, adorned his cars with steer horns, and wore a tattoo of a dagger with a snake coiled around it on his forearm. More importantly, Silas was known for his cold and intense eyes. Those who testified against him in the trial that finally sent him to prison told how intimidating it was to be sitting in front of his intense, rarely-blinking, cold eyes as he attempted to burn holes in the witnesses from his seat at the defense table.

The man who was Silas' younger brother, George, seemed built to be his opposite. George was skinny and slight. By all accounts, he was an affable person, easy to get along with and a pleasant person. In short, George was a businessman. His brother, however, was a shark in human skin.

Silas was born on July 3, 1907, and he was the fourth child and the first of eventually four boys. His father's name was Arthur and his mother was Katherine. Eventually Arthur and Katherine split and Katherine began to fancy a man named George W. Spunner, a lawyer. Katherine gave birth to another boy whom she named George William Jayne. Despite the last name of Spunner for the boy's father, she gave him the name of Jayne. Silas now had a brother and Katherine was still hoping to avoid a scandal.

Silas began getting into trouble at an early age. At seventeen, he was charged with rape, and his mother's lover, George

Spunner, represented him in court. The defense must not have been very good, however, because Si was convicted. According to reports from the time, Spunner actually seemed relieved when Silas was carted off behind a wall. Some have suggested that this was the time when Silas began to hate his brother.

The Jayne brothers, whatever their faults, were considered outstanding horsemen. All of the brothers began to ride professionally. Once Silas was released from jail, he went into the horse stable business with his brothers DeForest and Frank. By the time the 1930s came around, the Jaynes owned a ranch just outside of Woodstock, Illinois. The business was a success and entire trainloads of horses were being shipped around the country, with most of them becoming dog food. The brothers were horse drivers and drove their herds of horses through Woodstock to the trains waiting to take them to places where they would be slaughtered.

The brothers created quite a reputation for themselves in Woodstock, especially when they would drive their horses through town. They were loud and rough. They gained the nickname of "The Jesse Jayne Gang."

Among the brothers, it was DeForest who was considered the most talented. He gained a reputation for being an outstanding trick rider and an excellent riding instructor. DeForest also began to take a liking to the brother George and took him under his wing. By all reports, DeForest and George were very close, and DeForest did the best he could to control his brothers and was well liked by all of them and the people in the community.

However, DeForest was also in love with a woman named Mae Sweeney. They were in love to the point that they were engaged to be married. Mae had been one of DeForest's riding students, but she had serious problems mentally. She killed herself by drinking arsenic.

31

DeForest, the stabilizing force amongst "The Jesse Jayne Gang" was devastated beyond repair by this death. The family attended Mae's funeral and saw her put into the ground. The very next day DeForest woke, put on his best riding clothes, went to the cemetery, and put the twelve-gauge shotgun he had brought along with him into his mouth. He killed himself in front of the fresh dirt over Mae's grave.

With DeForest gone, Silas became a wild child. It also may have re-ignited the feelings of hatred and resentment between Silas and George. One of the things that DeForest did when he died was leave his favorite brother, George, twenty acres of land. Silas felt cheated by that and his hatred for his brother grew.

World War II broke out and Si, a convicted felon, was not allowed to join the Army. With that taken away from him, he turned his gang toward making money by selling horsemeat as beef. Since beef was being rationed during the war, they turned a handsome profit. During this time Silas also met people involved in Chicago crime, known as "The Outfit," and these bonds were forged, tested, and strengthened throughout his life.

During that time George was also in the horse business with his brothers, including Si. Things were not smooth between them, however. Silas continued to nurture his grudge against the brother he felt was a favorite. At one point, Silas turned a vicious Doberman on George and George had to beat the animal off with a cane. Si stood on the porch of his home and laughed.

The life of horsemen was one filled with money and high stakes. It was easy to make a lot of money, and very easy to lose everything. Owners of show horses often forked over tens of thousands of dollars for animals and then had to foot the bill for the training and housing of the animal. Show horses and the owning and training of those animals is a place where the rich like to hang out, and it is a particular passion of the rich daughters of the rich men who could afford to buy those horses. Despite it being considered folly of the rich, the men involved in buying, selling, and trading these horses is a deadly serious business.

At the horse shows, the winning is more about bragging rights than it is about the prize money, but the prize money can run into the hundreds of thousands of dollars. The animals themselves are often traded or bought and sold before and after shows. The price of the horses are often determined by how well they performed that very day, perhaps just minutes before the money changed hands. It was within this world that George and Silas entered once World War II was over.

Despite his intimidating look and his rough attitude, Si was a man who had an instinct about horses. Therefore, whatever he may have lacked in manners and style, he made up for in picking animals that would win shows and make money. Silas could be incredibly charming when he needed to be and often knew how to ingratiate himself with those rich men's daughters. It wasn't long, however, before his criminal mind figured out a way to turn those talents into a way of making money.

Silas soon developed a scam where he would greatly exaggerate the price of a horse. He would do this by showing a horse to the young twelve or thirteen-year-old daughter of one of the rich men he had marked. He would then tell the father he felt the daughter had some real talent with horses. Before the rich man knew what was happening, he had a daughter who was begging him for a horse. Silas would indicate that the horse was worth about $1,500 and, when the daughter had begged to the point the man was willing to pay, the horse's value would suddenly jump to $20,000.

Silas and his people also took the opportunity with these

33

young girls to indulge in truly depraved activities. They would offer to train them how to ride and then take advantage of them. Silas would introduce them to sex and would then brag to others about the girl he had bedded. If the girl complained, he would threaten to humiliate her by claiming she had been sleeping around with everyone at the stable. Even parents who had approached Silas with threats to go to the police would often shut up after being told something like that in order to protect their daughter's reputation. There were even cases when Silas never touched the girl in question, but he would threaten to leak a rumor about her promiscuity anyway.

Silas also used his intimidating methods to further his ambitions for money and power. He was not above doing acts of violence to gain more money. For example, there was a man named Dr. Thomas Phillips who ran a hospital for horses. Silas came to him back in 1967 and told him he needed to certify that a horse that was about to be purchased was healthy. Phillips looked at X-rays of the horse and felt that the horse was arthritic and lame. Apparently Silas had injected the horse with a drug to mask the pain before the potential buyer showed up to make it seem like it wasn't lame. Phillips refused to sign the form declaring the horse as healthy.

According to Phillips, he told Silas Jayne to go to hell and get out of his office. Silas had offered him five percent of the transaction that would have sold the lame horse. Silas was not willing to make another offer. Not long after he told Silas to get out of his office, a bomb went off at the veterinarian's clinic and blew apart a section of the building. A phone call just after that suggesting that the next bomb would be at his house unless he changed his mind, scared Phillips and made him worry about his family, but the vet refused to change his mind or sign the paperwork. So, Phillips bought himself a handgun and began wearing it around his office in a shoulder holster. The police investigated the bombing but could find nothing to trace it to Silas Jayne and no one was ever arrested for the crime.

Silas Jayne was nothing if not ambitious. It wasn't enough just to bilk rich daughters out of their father's money. The Jayne Gang, like any criminal organization, was always looking for new endeavors to expand into. Silas had learned, at a young age, that fire could be a beneficial thing when it ripped through a series of stables owned by the family and killed a number of horses. Silas had seen the insurance payout this brought, and so the Jayne Gang moved into insurance fraud.

A series of fires at houses, barns, businesses, and other structures suddenly began popping up, wreaking untold damage to property. Horses were often burned alive in the barns, increasing the amount of money paid out by the insurance companies. However, it wasn't enough for Silas to set fire to his own property; he realized it was a good way to get a message across to his potential enemies.

Soon, anyone who crossed Silas and his gang was likely to find their garage, property, or belongings burned. He also used bombs to create fear. One man attempted to sue Silas over the sale of a lame horse but soon dropped the case when a bomb exploded at a farmhouse he owned.

Silas employed people who were known to be connected with the Chicago Mob. Curtis Hansen was one of Si's trusted colleagues and he was rumored to be an enforcer and hit man for the Catura crime family, which was located in Chicago Heights. Despite this, the mob tended to give Silas a wide berth. Silas dealt in horses rather than gambling, prostitution, or drugs, which was what the mob was interested in—so they left him alone. Plus, it was rumored that the mob found Silas a little too crazy and unstable, even for their own ranks.

By the time 1952 came around, Si had established a profitable gang. He was running schemes almost constantly and his gang was going right along with him. At the same time, his brother George was moving away from Si's activities, trying to set out on his own. Apparently, the final straw for George came when Silas told him to break the leg of an otherwise healthy horse. George couldn't and wouldn't do that, and this further enraged his brother. George broke off on his own and even borrowed money from Silas to purchase the Happy Day Stables for his own purposes.

George may have made a mistake, at that time, that would end up being fatal. He decided to start breeding and showing his own show horses. In short, he decided to become a direct competitor against his brother. He was now a rival for business Silas desired—and this made him an enemy.

It turned out George had talents on par, perhaps better, than his brother. He had a knack for finding quality horses, a knack for training them, and a knack for finding talent to ride them. By the late 1950s, George was winning shows, and it was starting to affect his brother in the place he cared about most—in his wallet. In 1961, George's daughter beat out one of Silas' riders and Silas exploded at his brother, shouting, "I'll never talk to you again, you bastard!"

At that point, as far as Silas Jayne was concerned, his brother George was "Public Enemy Number One" and his attacks against George quickly escalated. George's office was burglarized. Someone loosened the lug nuts on George's truck when he was at the Ohio State Fair. Once that happened, George began to surround himself with tight security and he started carrying a gun. Death threats started soon after that and became a regular occurrence.

Things escalated to even more dangerous levels in 1963. By that time, George had managed to lure away one of Silas' top riders, a talented woman named Cheryl Lynn Rude. Rude, riding one of George's horses, beat out Silas' horses at the Cin-

cinnati Horse Show. One month later, Rude was walking with George out to his barn to look at some horses when George realized he had parked his Cadillac in front of the barn the night before. He handed the keys to Rude and asked her to move the car away from the door. As soon as Rude turned the key in the ignition, sticks of dynamite, strapped beneath the car and wired to the ignition, went off.

The explosion knocked George to the ground. The blast tore apart a large portion of the barn. Beneath the car, a crater was formed. Inside the care, Cheryl Rude was blown to pieces. As soon as it happened and the incident was reported, the police zeroed in on the feud between George and his brother. They even focused in on one of Silas' men, a man named James Blottiaux as the likely man who planted the bomb. Just as he was about to be brought up on charges, however, key evidence suddenly vanished from the Chicago Police Department evidence room. The case was dropped, for the time being.

Just five days after Rude was blown to pieces, two men whom Silas had hired to kill George got cold feet about the deal they had made and approached George instead, they told George that Silas had offered them $15,000 to do the job. George sent the two men to the police to tell their story.

At the same time, three young women who were horse enthusiasts disappeared. Ann Miller, 21, Patty Blough, 19, and Renee Bruhl, 19, were last seen entering a blue and white colored speedboat while visiting the Indiana Dunes State Park. They have long been considered murdered and authorities have often guessed that they may have seen the man who planted the bomb on George's car and that Silas may have decided they needed to disappear. To this date, no one has ever been charged with their disappearances and their bodies have never been found.

The police set up a sting operation to try and get some dirt on Silas. They put a wire on one of the men he had hired to kill George and managed to get Silas on tape ordering the death of his brother. One of the men, Stephen Grod, explained that Silas had given him $1,000 as a down payment on the job. Silas was indicted on a conspiracy to commit murder charge and Grod was to be their star witness.

However, when Grod entered the courtroom during the trial and took the witness stand, his memory suddenly failed him. He claimed he remembered nothing about any $1,000. He also said he had no memory of Silas talking about killing his brother or hiring anyone to accomplish the job. Grod was sentenced to thirty days in jail for contempt. The recording also managed to disappear and the case against Silas fell apart.

Years later, the case was re-opened by federal authorities after they had succeeded in closing the Schuessler-Peterson murders. With Silas gone, they figured someone might step forward to spill about Rude's murder. Eventually they found enough evidence to convict Blottiaux of the murder and were able to prove that Silas had paid him $10,000 to put the dynamite on George's car. An exact motive for the crime was never established, but by this time it was well known how much Silas hated George. Others have suggested it was an attempt to silence George because he knew of Silas' involvement in the Schuessler-Peterson murders. Blottiaux is still serving 100 to 300 years in prison.

George was, understandably, shaken after the bombing incident. A friend of George's suggested to him that he hire a hit man and take out Silas before Silas managed to do the same to him. George wasn't willing to go that far, but he did start to take precautions. He refused to eat at the same restaurant twice, for example, and began starting his car by keeping his feet out of the open door so any blast would send him out of the car instead of through the roof. When he appeared at horse shows, he would walk into the ring with a horse on either side of him in case a sniper had been hired to take him out during the show.

George was still hopeful that he could build a bridge toward his brother. At a family reunion in 1967, he negotiated a deal with his brother in which he would quit competing in shows against him. Not long after that, when his daughters were about to marry, he paid Silas a huge amount of money in hopes that Si would not disrupt the ceremonies. George also began looking for other ways to keep an eye on Silas, and one of them backfired horribly.

George thought that one of the best ways to keep himself safe was to keep track of Silas. He had a transmitter attached to his brother's car. Whenever Silas was near, a receiver George kept with him would start to beep. Eventually, the device stopped working and George figured the battery in it needed replacing. So, George tried taking a page out of his brother's book and hired an ex-con named Frank Michelle to sneak onto Silas' property and change the battery on the transmitter. Michelle was driven to the property by his own wife and family.

Michelle managed to sneak onto Silas' property, but he was not undetected. Silas' dogs sniffed him out and chased the man. Silas came out with a gun and shot the man to death as he attempted to climb over a fence.

When the police arrived, Silas claimed it was self-defense. He stated that Michelle had walked up to his front door, rang the doorbell, and then fired at him right through the door. Silas stated he reached for an M-1 carbine and ran after Michelle. He then told police that from a distance of about eight feet, he fired the entire clip into Michelle. Michelle's body was riddled with nine bullets. Si managed to convince the authorities that his version of the story was true and, with no other witnesses to the event to be found, they could not bring any charges against the man.

Many years later, long after Silas was dead, the government's

Bureau of Alcohol, Tobacco, and Firearms was able to produce some witnesses to the events who told a decidedly different story. According to these men, Michelle had been caught on the property and dragged to a remote spot where he was brutally tortured. His genitals were crushed with a pair of pliers and other tortures were heaped upon him. Eventually, having grown bored with the game, Silas and two other of his men shot Michelle as he begged for his life.

Silas was now angrier and more determined than ever to end the life of his brother. He began to look for someone else to take out George. He turned to a man in his employ, a former police officer named Edwin Nefeld, and asked him to find a man to do the job. Nefeld, in turn, found a man named Melvin Adams.

Adams was a building engineer and had never killed anyone in his life. He had once pulled a gun on a man, but he never pulled the trigger. Apparently, word of his gun-showing incident had spread, giving him a reputation that brought him to the attention of Nefeld and Silas. Adams agreed to meet with Silas in a southern Chicago suburb called Harvey.

At that meeting, Silas appeared to be in a great mood and, evidently, was in quite a mood to share with Adams. He told him that he had been trying to kill George for ten years at that point. He also was quick to give Adams several tips on how he could best go about killing George. One suggestion he offered was to machine-gun George's car while it was driving down the highway. Another idea Si liked was using a bomb to blow him to pieces. Silas also stressed to Adams that no witnesses should be left alive if they were around when he killed George. And he explained that this meant George's wife and children if they happened to be around.

Silas assured Adams that he would take care of everything. He offered $20,000 for the job and promised he would provide any guns or lawyers Adams would need. Adams agreed to the deal.

Melvin Adams began following George around. He tailed George to horse shows and across the country. He even once walked right up to George's home but he found himself unable to pull the trigger at that time. Later, he stated that when he walked up to the house, George was there and less than two feet from him—and that George was alone. Adams realized that the consequences of crossing that line could be the step he didn't really want to take and couldn't bring himself to pull out his gun and fire.

Adams tried to back out of the deal. He had another meeting with Silas and told him that it was too difficult. He stated that George was too difficult to find alone and too heavily guarded. Silas refused to accept that Adams could not do the job and added another $10,000 to the price of the job. Silas also suggested that Adams get some help and Adams turned to a co-worker named Julius Barnes to help with the job.

On October 28, 1970, George Jayne was celebrating his son's sixteenth birthday. It was a quiet family affair. George, his son, daughters, and wife were sitting in their basement playing cards when Melvin Adams and Julius Barnes drove up to their home. It was Barnes who stepped out of the car and walked up to the house. Moments later a shot blasted through the basement window and George slumped over at the table in front of his family.

This would prove to be the final crime that Silas could not manage to worm, bribe, or threaten his way out of, however. In fact, from the get-go Silas was the prime suspect, as his feud with his brother was well known to almost everyone in the suburbs. Plus, George had been preparing for this eventuality for much of his adult life. No sooner had George died, letters he had written in the event of his death began to appear. In each letter, George stated that Silas had been trying to kill him for years and that he feared that, inevitably, he would succeed in his task.

George's wife, Marion, had her own lists of suspects. She approached Melvin Adams and showed him a bag that held $25,000. She offered him that money in exchange for information that would lead to the killer of her husband. She begged him to tell the authorities who had committed this crime. It was too much for Adams to bear and he finally caved in. He visited the Illinois Bureau of Investigation and began to talk. He told his story in exchange for immunity.

In addition to Adams, the authorities named Barnes, Nefeld, Silas and Joseph LaPalca as codefendants. Adams was the one given immunity and he immediately began telling authorities all they needed to know to bring the rest of the crew to trial. The trial itself lasted a month and Adams was the star witness for the prosecution. Many who attended the trial talked about how intense Silas' eyes were, and how intimidating he was whenever anyone was speaking against him. This time, though, no one went missing, and no one changed their stories. Silas and his cohorts were convicted.

Silas Jayne and Joseph LaPalca, another member of his crew, were sentenced to six to twenty years on conspiracy to commit murder. Barnes was convicted of murder and sentenced to fifteen to thirty-five years. Silas went off to the Vienna Correctional Center.

As for Adams, he never did collect the money Marion had offered him. He felt he didn't deserve the money after what he had done and had been a part of.

Silas spent seven years in prison. From behind those prison walls, he still managed to control his empire. He was able to get advice and counsel to members of his crew about their schemes and activities. He had trained them all well, and they continued to steal the money of wealthy women for worthless horses and bilk insurance companies out of thousands of dollars.

In January of 1979, Silas Jayne stepped out of prison a free man. He held an interview with a local newspaper claiming, yet again, that he had nothing to do with the death of his brother. He also stated he would use his money, influence, and resources to try and track down the real killer of his brother—and that he hoped his troubles with the law were over.

However, just seven months after he was released, a grand jury indicted him for plotting an arson the killed thirty-three show horses from within his prison cell. The case was based mostly on testimony from one of Si's former cellmates. This same man also stated Silas kept a "hit list" of people he felt he needed to kill, including George's wife, Marion, her daughter, and Melvin Adams. Once again, however, Silas managed to beat these charges and was not sent back to prison.

Silas spent the rest of his life attempting to appear as though he were living a quiet, modest life in the suburbs. Although he was rumored and known by many to be a millionaire, his reported income was around $5,000. He was never brought up on charges of income tax evasion.

Silas was eventually diagnosed with leukemia. Despite this, he is believed to have been instrumental in the disappearance and death of candy heiress Helen Brach, which was to be his last scheme. Silas Jayne died quietly, to the surprise of almost everyone, in his bed, from leukemia, on July 13, 1987. These days, his stables are gone and the name of the Jayne Gang has faded from memory, at least from the memory of the general public.

Anyone whoever met Silas Jayne, or knew anyone who was affected by any of his schemes, however, still remembers the man—well.

Chapter Four
A Tenuous Connection and Another Horrific Crime

The next crime that anyone sees with the name Silas Jayne attached seems to be the one that is the least likely that he had any actual involvement. It is, however, one of the most-famous unsolved crimes in the history of Chicago. It bears many resemblances to the Schuessler-Peterson murders and occurred at almost exactly the same time. In fact, the similarities in the crimes and the timing were such that much of the city assumed they were related and it sent Chicago into another spasm of terror.

It was December 28, 1956, and Patricia and Barbara Grimes wanted to see the latest Elvis movie playing at a theater only a mile away from their home. The two girls loved Elvis and had seen *Love Me Tender* ten times. Patricia was thirteen years old and Barbara was fifteen, and despite this, their parents didn't have a problem letting them see the movie by themselves.

At 9:00 p.m., they were spotted and recognized in the line at the theater to buy popcorn. At 11:00 p.m., the two girls were spotted by reliable witnesses on the Archer Avenue bus. Those two witness reports are the last times anyone can ever be sure that Barbara and Patricia Grimes were seen alive.

What happened next plunged the city into a panic and the news of the missing girls spread across the country. Elvis himself made a plea for the girl's safe return once word leaked that they were avid fans of the King. There would also be accusations of botched police work and a very controversial autopsy report that would serve only to add more questions than it answered. Mixed in with this complex cauldron is a passing mention of the ruthless horseman Silas Jayne.

The two girls' mother, Loretta, began to get worried about her daughters by 11:30 p.m., even though she later told the police she had not expected them home until 11:45 p.m. Once midnight came and went, Ms. Grimes began to panic and she sent her seventeen-year-old daughter, Theresa, and her son, Joey, to the bus stop where the girls were expected to appear. The two of them waited for three buses and when their sisters still did not appear, they returned home. No one else in the Grimes family ever saw the girls alive again.

Others, however, began to come forward insisting they had seen the girls alive and well and all over the city. Classmates of the two girls insisted they had seen both sisters at Angelo's Restaurant a full twenty-four hours after their disappearance was first reported. In another part of town, a railroad conductor insisted that he saw both girls on a train near the Great Lakes Naval Training Center in the far-northern suburbs of Glenview. A security guard, also on the northwest side of the city, gave directions to two girls he said he thought were Patricia and Barbara.

More witnesses, these on the first of January, came forward saying the two girls were on a CTA bus traveling down Damen Avenue. A man named George Pope, who worked at the Unity Hotel on 61st Street, said he turned away two girls who looked far too young, and then decided they looked like the Grimes sisters. Three employees at a store called Kresge stated they saw two girls, who looked exactly like the two girls missing, listening to Elvis Presley records on January 3rd.

The police traced every lead and person who came forward with a story. They could not prove that any of the stories above were viable or reasonable. As far as the police were concerned, however, the two girls had run away. Loretta refused to believe the girls had done so, and insisted that they were missing and that something foul was afoot.

The police launched the largest manhunt in the history of the city of Chicago. It was the Chicago police who got Elvis himself to make a statement asking the girls to return home. The police came up empty-handed.

The constant and conflicting stories were just some of the strange things the police had to deal with. A series of ransom notes began to show up at the door of Loretta Grimes. The notes were eventually proven to be fraudulent and from a mental patient, but not before Loretta Grimes traveled all the way to Milwaukee on January 12 to sit in a church indicated as an exchange point in the letters. She had $1,000 on the bench beside her and waited for, what the letter promised would be a visit from Barbara who would collect the money, deliver it, and then release her sister. Loretta Grimes sat there for a very long time and no one every showed.

Then, on January 14, came one of the eeriest incidents in the entire case. The phone rang at the house of Wallace and Ann Tollstan, whose daughter, Sandra, was a friend and classmate of Patricia Grimes. The first call came in around midnight. Mr. Tollstan was jolted right out of his sleep and scrambled for the phone. He heard someone on the other end, but when he said *hello*, the person did not respond. He could hear someone at the other end, but when they continued to remain silent he hung up. Fifteen minutes later, the phone rang again and this time, Mrs. Tollstan answered the phone.

This time the voice on the other end spoke and asked, "Is that you Sandra? Is Sandra there?" Mrs. Tollstan tried to awaken her daughter and get her to the phone but, before she could do this, the person on the other end of the line had hung up. Mrs. Tollstan was certain, and she told police as much, that the voice on the other end was Patricia Grimes.

On January 15, the police received a call from a man who declined and then refused to identify himself. He kept repeating that he had seen the bodies of the two girls in a park at 81st and Wolf. He also stated this information had come to him in a dream and then he hung up. The police traced the call to Green's Liquor Market and the cops found the caller was Walter Kranz, a steamfitter. He was eventually taken into custody, once the bodies of the two girls were found, but the police couldn't connect him to the crime.

All questions about the fate of the Grimes sisters ended on January 22nd, when Leonard Prescott, a construction worker, spotted something strange on the side of the road. He was driving south on German Church Road when he saw clothing and what he thought was two discarded store mannequins near a guardrail not far from the road. Just a few more feet further, the land dropped away into Devil's Creek. Prescott continued home, shaken and unsure of what he had seen. He grabbed his wife and asked her to come back with him to the spot on German Church Road to confirm what he had seen. She did and they called the police. The bodies of Barbara and Patricia Grimes had been found, discarded, nude, frozen, and left on the side of the road.

Sheriff Joseph D. Lohman and an investigator from the Coroner's Office, Harry Glos, along with some other official in charge of the investigation, concluded that the two girls had been lying beside the road for several days and maybe as far back as January 9. The bodies had been dusted with snow, and this was the date of the last snowfall.

The news of the discovery of the bodies hit the newspapers. It wasn't long before reporters and the public were trying to draw connections between the Grimes sister murders and the Schuessler-Peterson murders.

Barbara Grimes was found lying on her side with her legs drawn up toward her body. Barbara's head was covered by the body of Patricia, who was lying on her back. Patricia's head was turned to the right. They looked as though they had been discarded like trash out of the window of a moving car. They were both nude.

The discovery of the bodies sent the police into action. For a massive search of the woods, 162 officers from Chicago, Cook County, the Forest Preserve police and officials, and five south suburban police departments converged on the area where the bodies had been located. It was too much and there were too many people. The officers, attempting to help, began trampling and stepping on potentially vital evidence. In addition to the police, word had spread, and reporters, medical examiners, and onlookers began to walk all over the area as well. In short, the crime scene was already completely corrupted and almost useless, just like the crime scene had become during the Schuessler-Peterson investigation years before.

This was just the tip of the iceberg for how badly things would go for this investigation. Things were just going to get more confusing from there as the autopsies on the bodies of the two girls were performed. The bodies had been taken to the Cook County Morgue where they were to be stored until they could be thawed out enough for the autopsies to occur.

The movement of the corpses was mishandled from the get-go, however. Various police investigators and reporters both got a very close look at the bodies. Before too long, reports of the condition of the bodies were leaking to the public. The story that was published described bruises and marks on the bodies of the two young women. According to one account, Patricia had particularly "ugly" wounds to her abdomen. The same story also described the left side of her face as being battered and the nose as broken. The reporters also stated Barbara's face as battered, bruised, and broken, and that they were puncture wounds in her chest, possibly from an ice pick. No explanations were evident for these wounds and none have ever been offered to this day.

The day after the bodies were removed, they were deemed thawed enough for autopsies to be performed. It was hoped that this would shed some new light on the crime, but those hopes were soon dashed. In fact, the autopsies, performed by three talented and experienced pathologists, would only add confusion and lead to more problems in the investigation. None of the three pathologists could agree on what had happened to the girls or what had killed them. They could not agree on a time of death and only reached a final consensus on the reason for their deaths by eliminating all other causes.

The report stated Barbara and Patricia Grimes had died of shock and exposure, and not wounds to their abdomens, chests, or heads. The pathologists also agreed on a date of death of December 28, which was the same night the two disappeared. This left everyone confused because it did not explain the other reports and sightings of the girls, nor did it explain why no one had seen the bodies since that date, considering they were not very far from the side of the road.

Barbara and Patricia Grimes were finally laid to rest on January 28. It had been exactly one month since they had last been seen alive by their family. It was exactly one month since they had disappeared. It was one month after they had been reported missing and the police were nowhere near solving the case or finding their killers.

The Chicago Police and other investigators launched into high gear. In fact, the murders of the two women became an obsession among lawmen and citizens alike. Local communities organized searches to look for clues. These groups passed out flyers and began questioning people for information. Some communities raised money to donate to the Grimes family, which ultimately was used to pay off the home they had on Damen Avenue.

Meanwhile, the local newspaper, the *Chicago Tribune*, invited its readers to send in their theories about the case. To encourage submissions, they offered $50 for any theory they published. St. Maurice's Church offered $1,000 as a reward and advertised this by sending out letters and flyers to residents. Photographs of the girls' friends dressed in clothing similar to what the girls had last been seen wearing were sent out and distributed around the city in hopes the pictures might jog someone's memory.

The killer still remained at large, however. The police called in and questioned an amazing 300,000 people. Of those, 2,000 were very seriously considered as potential suspects and interrogated seriously. One of those considered early on was, as mentioned, was Walter Kranz who had called in with his tip from a dream back on January 15, since the bodies had been found not very far from where he said they would be found. He was interrogated several times and took several lie detector tests, but none of them showed guilt and there was no evidence to link him with the crime.

Another suspect was a seventeen-year-old man named Max Fleig. At that time, however, juveniles were not allowed to be hooked up to the lie detector machine. Despite the law against this, Fleig was persuaded to take the test anyway. During this investigation, Fleig reportedly confessed to kidnapping the sisters. Despite this information, because the test was not legal, it could not be used against Fleig and he was let go. Several years later Max Fleig would end up sent to prison for the murder of a young woman.

It is in this massive search that the name of Silas Jayne comes up according to some accounts. However, this is also where things get very uncertain and murky as far as Silas is concerned. In fact, it seems as though his association with the case has come into being because of a book that mentioned the case in connection with tales of ghosts.

Of course, the area on German Church Road where the bodies of the two girls were found has gained a reputation for being haunted. A house nearby was abandoned by the owners shortly after the bodies were found and, reportedly, remained so for many years. Reports of strange noises have been frequently heard by curiosity seekers, ghost-hunters, and would-be investigators for years.

A book came out not too long ago that discussed the case. Within the telling of the tale of the Grime sisters, it mentions a man named "Silas Jane" confessed to the crime and was interrogated by police. The storyteller even goes so far as to declare this "Silas Jane" as a horse breeder. In addition to the misspelling of the last name, there are more things that seem vastly out of character for the notorious criminal and horseman.

In every other case when Silas Jayne was accused of a crime, witnesses would be bought off or they would simply disappear. He drilled into his crew and the people who worked for him that they were to remain silent. He paid off potential witnesses and threatened them. In short, having Silas Jayne come out of the woodwork and suddenly confess to one of the most notorious crimes and brutal murders in the history of the city seems drastically out of character and bizarre. The only possible explanation would be if Silas Jayne felt like deliberately messing with the police and throwing off the investigation. However, considering how brutal interrogation methods were at the time, it again seems very out of place.

The other problem with the story is that it has become impossible to corroborate. Looking for newspaper clips of the crime could not find any quote indicating that Silas Jayne had confessed or been brought in for questioning. However, several web sites about the crime seem to have picked up on the story printed in the haunted house book and have reported it as fact. There is even one web site which states that Silas Jane was a drifter, while another says that the Silas Jane mentioned was actually the wealthy horse breeder.

The original book goes on to say that Silas eventually admitted he had made up the entire confession. Once again, however, no explanation for why he would do this is given.

It seems possible that confusion has grown over the Grimes sisters' murders and the murders of the three boys from a few years before that. Perhaps someone, while researching one, assumed Silas was also involved in the other. As to whether or not Silas Jayne confessed, or was even interrogated about the crimes, it is unknown. As was mentioned earlier, in a net that brought in over 300,000 people, it seems possible he might have been questioned. He was known to be a criminal. There were rumors of his involvement in the murder of the three boys, but no evidence. It may be possible he was questioned.

Regardless of whether or not Silas Jayne had anything to do with the murders of the two girls, or if he was even questioned, what is known is that the Grime sisters' murder remains one of the most notorious in the history of the city of Chicago. As the police continued to question seemingly everyone who was alive at the time and living in the city, they had to deal with more nuts, cranks, false confessions, and supposed psychics with visions of the killer or killers.

The Cook County Sheriff Joseph Lohman arrested a man from Tennessee who was known as a drifter. He was named

Edward L. "Benny" Bedwell. He had hair styled after Elvis and sideburns. One report had come in that he had been seen with the Grimes sisters in a restaurant where he was employed as a dishwasher. During questioning, Bedwell admitted he had met and spoken to two girls during his time working at the restaurant, but stated the two girls were not the Grimes sisters.

The investigators brought in the owners of the restaurant, John and Minnie Duros. The two of them stated on the morning of December 30, a group of people entered the restaurant including two young girls. The two owners described the taller of the two girls as being so drunk or perhaps sick that she staggered when she walked. The two girls sat in a booth and listened to songs by Elvis on the jukebox before heading outside.

Minnie Duros described how the two girls hung out outside the restaurant for a while before the taller girl returned to the booth, sat down and put her head down on the table. The other girl wanted her to get into the car, but she refused to go. Eventually, the other girl and two men came inside and insisted the tall girl get into the car. Minnie herself stepped in and suggested that they leave the girl alone because she appeared to be sick, but the entire group left the restaurant anyway. As they left, the shorter of the two women stated they were sisters.

Minnie Duros was absolutely certain that the two girls she had seen and spoken to were the Grimes sisters. So certain was her identification that Lohman became convinced the story was true. Lohman also factored in the fact that Bedwell so resembled Elvis that this might have made him particularly attractive to the two girls. Finally, Bedwell himself gave graphic details of sex and perversion regarding the two women he said he had met, but insisted were not the Grimes sisters. Lohman felt he finally had found the man who had ended the life of Barbara and Patricia Grimes.

The problem was that no one else involved in the investigation believed that Bedwell was the killer. Bedwell made and then recanted his confession three times and then re-enacted the crime in front of Lohman. Lohman decided to book Bedwell on a charge of murder despite the fact that the confessions and Bedwell's story had more holes in it than a leaky boat. His story was inconsistent, vague, and contradicted itself, plus, there were accusations that his confession had been beaten out of him. In fact, Bedwell himself, on January 31, stated that he had made the confession because men working with Lohman had beaten him and threatened him during their questioning.

Harry Glos, another investigator, thought that it might have been possible that Bedwell was involved in some way with the crime but that the charges, his story, and his overall appearance made him an unlikely suspect. The State's Attorney, a man named Benjamin Adamowski, agreed with that assessment and he ordered the charges be dropped and that Bedwell be released. Bedwell left the courtroom and was immediately arrested on a warrant from the state of Florida for the rape of a thirteen-year-old girl. It was another charge Bedwell managed to get out of because of the amount of time between the supposed crime and his arrest. The similarities between the crime in Florida and the Grimes case were disturbing.

According to the thirteen year old who had accused him, Bedwell had kidnapped her and held her captive for three days. She eventually escaped and notified police. Bedwell ran and had been missing until news of his arrest in Illinois spread across the country. Eventually, Bedwell would be arrested on a weapons charge and put in prison where he would die in 1986.

When Bedwell was dismissed, it brought about another session of investigating bodies arguing with each other over the direction of the investigation. The entire case began to get bogged down in red tape and stagnation. Things went from bad to worse when Harry Glos began to publicly criticize the autopsy findings. He particularly criticized the official cause and time of death. He made a public statement saying that it was impossible for Barbara and Patricia to have been killed on the night the coroner's report said it had happened. In his opinion, the layer of ice on the bodies of the two girls proved that they had been warm when they were left beside the road and that only after January 7 had there been enough snow to generate the ice. He also brought up the puncture wounds and bruises that the reporters had noted on the bodies.

Glos stated he was certain the two girls had been treated violently and had, therefore, died violently. He also made statements that at least one of the girls, most likely the older sister, Barbara, had been sexually violated before she died. At first, the pathologists who had performed the autopsies denied this, but when Glos persisted, they finally relented and admitted that it was true. They also stated they had kept the information secret in order to use it against potential suspects in questioning.

Glos' statements infuriated the coroner's office, and the coroner, William McCarron, had Glos fired. Sheriff Lohman then stepped in and deputized Glos. Glos would continue to work on the case without pay. Lohman also felt that the girls had been victims of a sexual predator and had died violently. Of course, until his death in 1969, Lohman was also convinced that Bedwell had killed the two girls.

In subsequent years, investigators have theorized that the two girls may have run into Bedwell and perhaps another man who may have been older than Bedwell. Rumors began to circulate that the police had covered up parts of the girl's social lives to make them seem more innocent than they actually were. One rumor was that they were often seen hanging out at a bar and accepting drinks bought for them by much older men. One theory was that one of those men might have been Bedwell.

Glos himself stated that he had proof from medical exams of the bodies that at least one of the girls was sexually active. Investigators who have looked at slides of tissue samples from the girls since then have stated that both girls were probably sexually active. It has been stated, as well, that this information was withheld to spare the Grimes' family further grief.

Even today, the case is still listed as open. Detectives who have been on the force for years have taken their turns with the case. One investigator said that the story of the two sisters was probably more broad and far-reaching that anyone ever theorized. One has suggested that the girls were probably abducted by a man running a "white slavery" ring. They were taken to the woods as part of this and when they had refused to participate in prostitution they were strangled. Another suggestion in the same vein is that friends of the two girls may have lured them into prostitution and when they realized exactly what was expected of them and tried to get out of it, they were killed to keep things quiet.

There are many, even to this day, who refuse to believe that the girls had anything to do with prostitution or white slavery. In fact, for some, the mere mention of the possibility will get you an angry response. Those who adhere to this belief find it more comforting that two teenage girls simply ran across the wrong people that night and ended up dead on the side of the road. For them, the idea of a "stranger danger" is a better idea than kids who may have been actively involved in things that lead to their demise.

Years have passed. The case has remained open, but as the years go by, it seems less and less likely that anyone will ever be caught or brought to justice for the crimes. Loretta Grimes, the poor sad mother, was reportedly a broken woman from that point forward. She was a shallow shell of what she had been. She passed away in December of 1989. At one point, a $100,000 reward was posted for a solution to the crime. Nothing ever came from that either.

Hope was again reached when the case of the three boys was re-opened. Suddenly a killer in a decades-old crime from the 50s was solved and the killer was sent to prison. The name of Silas Jayne and his people was brought up again. Some thought that maybe the man sent to prison for murdering those three boys might have some knowledge or involvement in the deaths of Barbara and Patricia. Sadly, this seems not to have been the case.

Today, all that is left is the spot where the two naked bodies were found. It has grown in legend just like the murder itself. The house that stood nearby has been torn down and only the empty foundation exists. Some say the entire area is haunted and that phantom cars and mysterious noises like tires squealing, doors opening, and objects being tossed over the guard rail can be heard.

Whatever is or is not happening on German Church Road these days is really irrelevant. What is known is that two young girls were brutally murdered one night a long time ago. It turned the city upside down and may, or may not, have had an affect on Silas Jayne and his crew. No one has ever been brought to trial. No one has ever been convicted. Their murders remain unsolved.

Part Two
The Crime of the Century

An Introduction
The Bobby Franks Murder

In 1924, a young boy of fourteen named Bobby Franks was very brutally murdered on his way home from school. It was a crime that, once again, succeeded in shocking the normally gruff and blue-collar city of Chicago. However, the murder itself turned out to be just the starting point for a crime that would be called, at that time, the "Crime of the Century."

It turned out that two very young and intelligent young men from wealthy or well-to-do families felt that they were so bright they could easily commit murder. In fact, they attempted to commit the "perfect crime" as a kind of game. If this sounds familiar to you, then you may have seen the Alfred Hitchcock movie *Rope,* which was based on a play of the same name. Both the play and the movie take their story from the real life tale of Leopold and Loeb.

The case would electrify the entire nation. It would also introduce the world to the famous and charismatic lawyer, Clarence Darrow, who would go on to even greater fame during the "Scopes Monkey Trial" not long after.

It is an early tale of wasted youth by wealthy young people with too much money, little parental control, and too much time on their hands. Sadly, it is a tale that would be repeated and repeated throughout the rest of the century and into the current one. There would be many "Trials" and "Crimes of the Century" after this one, but this was one of the first and still, all these years later, one of the strangest.

Chapter Five
The Perfect Crime

It was Wednesday night, May, 21, 1924, and in the Franks house, Jacob and Flora had just had dinner. Neither of them had been able to eat much. Their son, Bobby, was supposed to have been home from school hours ago. He had planned on walking home by himself, as he had done many times before, but he had never shown up. His brother and sister, Jack and Josephine, were less worried. They thought he might have simply gone out with some friends or over to a friend's house.

The Franks family were not overly wealthy. They were hardly as rich as some in the Chicago area, like Marshall Fields or Montgomery Ward. They were not poor either, however. In our modern vocabulary, we could probably declare them "middle class."

Bobby attended a decent school. His friends were all well-bred. His brother and sister thought Bobby might have gone over to a friend's house to play tennis. And one of those family friends belonged to the Loeb family. Bobby's father could see the Loeb's home from his window and looked over there to see if his son was on the tennis courts, but they were empty.

Jacob decided it was time to call Bobby's school to see if Bobby was still there. Meanwhile, his wife, Flora, began asking Bobby's classmates if they had seen him. Once Jacob had determined that Bobby was not still at the school and had not gotten locked inside the building, he contacted a lawyer friend to find out what to do next. Jacob and his friend convinced the headmaster to let them search the school to see if Bobby was hidden inside.

Once Jacob and his friend left, the phone at the Franks'

house rang. Flora answered the phone. A man's voice spoke on the other end and identified himself as Johnson. He said, "Your son has been kidnapped. He is all right. There will be further news in the morning." With that Flora fainted dead away with the phone in her hand and laid there on the floor until her husband came home.

Flora and Jacob were unable to sleep, as you might imagine. Jacob's lawyer friend, Samuel Ettelson, also stayed there with them. At two in the morning, Ettelson and Jacob decided it would be best to notify the police. The two of them traveled to the nearest police station, but Ettelson realized that none of the police officers he knew were on duty at that time. Both men decided to head back to the Franks house and wait to see what would happen when the sun came up.

When morning came, so did a letter brought by a mailman. Jacob tore open the envelope and read the letter inside.

"Dear Sir:
As you no doubt know by this time, your son has been kidnapped. Allow us to assure you that he is, at present, well and safe. You need fear no physical harm for him, provided you live up carefully to the following instructions and to such others as you will receive by future communications. Should you, however, disobey any of our instructions, even slightly, his death will be the penalty.

1. For obvious reasons make absolutely no attempt to communicate with either police authorities or any private agency. Should you already have communicated with the police, allow them to continue their investigations, but do not mention this letter.
2. Secure before noon today $10,000. This money must be composed entirely of old bills of the following denominations: $2,000 in $20 bills, $8,000 in $50 bills. The money must be old. Any attempt to include new or marked bills will render the entire venture futile.
3. The money should be placed in a large cigar box, or if this is impossible, in a heavy cardboard box, securely closed and wrapped in white paper. The wrapping paper should be sealed at all openings with sealing wax.
4. Have the money with you, prepared as directed above, and

remain at home after one o'clock. See that the telephone is not in use."

The letter was signed by a man claiming to be George Johnson. It also indicated that as long as the money was delivered as instructed, Bobby would be returned to his home unharmed. Jacob read the letter, allowed Ettelson to read the letter, and then set about trying to secure the money.

While Jacob was off finding the $10,000, his friend Ettelson decided it was time to call his friend who was chief of detectives on the Chicago Police Department. At that same time, a newspaper reporter was tipped off to reports of a kidnapping involving the Franks family. Also at this time, he heard a story of the body of a young boy being found near Wolf Lake, which was being labeled as a possible drowning. The reporter managed to find Mr. Franks and give the description of the body to him, but Mr. Franks stated he didn't think it sounded like his son. Mr. Franks' brother-in-law was dispatched to view the body.

That afternoon, as had been promised in the letter, the phone rang and a man claiming to be George Johnson spoke to Ettelson. He told him that a Yellow Cab had been ordered to the Franks home. He was to get in and head to a drug store at 1465 East Sixty-third Street. Ettelson gave the phone to Jacob and the instructions were repeated. Due to the shock and sheer exhaustion experienced by both men, they forgot the address just given to them for the address of the store.

Terrified, shaking, heart pounding, Jacob replaced the phone only to feel it and hear it come to life again beneath his hand. Jacob picked up the phone and heard the voice of his brother-in-law. It was bad news. He had identified the body as that of Bobby Franks.

From that point forward it was no longer a missing persons

case, but a murder investigation. Unfortunately, the police were already off to a bad start because Mr. Franks and Ettelson could not remember the address that had been given to them. When a Yellow Cab showed up in front of the Franks house, the driver had been given no further instructions so the two men could not get to the drugstore.

As things were going badly at the Franks house, the kidnappers themselves had no idea that their plot had derailed and the true crime had been revealed. At the Van de Bogert & Ross Drugstore at East Sixty-third Street the phone rang. An employee at the store answered the ringing phone and a voice on the other end asked for Mr. Franks. He was told that there was no Mr. Franks present. Just a few minutes after that call the phone rang again. Once again, an employee answered and the request for Mr. Franks was repeated and a description of the man given. Once again, he was told that there was no one matching the name or description given.

Rewards were posted and leaked to the public. Mr. Franks offered $5,000 of his own money. Police Chief Morgan Collins stepped forward with a reward of $1,000. At the same time, the biggest newspapers in the city, the *Tribune* and *Herald Examiner*, each offered $5,000 for information leading to the people who kidnapped and murdered Bobby Franks.

At this point the State's Attorney, Robert Crowe, took over the investigation. He assigned an assistant named Bert Cronson to the case. Cronson was a nephew of Ettelson, the lawyer friend of Jacob Franks. There was a political motivation for Crowe to step in. He was trying to become a major force within the Chicago Republican Party and finding the killers quickly would do a lot toward that goal.

The investigators swarmed over the Wolf Lake culvert where the body had been found. Near the culvert were railroad tracks. Railroad workers had been the ones who had seen a naked boy in the water. Clothes belonging to Bobby Franks were found not far away. They investigators also found a pair of eyeglasses that did not belong to Bobby.

The police reviewed the typewritten ransom note. They determined that it had been typed by an inexperienced typist. The typewriter was an Underwood. The coroner made a statement that he felt the note was composed by someone with significant education because the sentence structure and the perfect English.

With the idea that the killer might have been educated caused the police to focus on three teachers at the school where Bobby Franks attended. The three teachers were brought in for questioning while the police searched their apartments. One teacher was released not long after being brought in and questioned. The other two teachers were to remain in police custody.

The police began to focus on the eyeglasses found at the scene. Not only did they not belong to Bobby, but they didn't belong to any of the teachers. The frames were made of a material known as Xylonite and appeared to have been chewed at the ends. The prescription itself was not unusual. Photos of the glasses were published in the newspapers while the police began to visit eye doctors in the area and visit optical companies that might have made the lenses and frames.

On May 23 a big break came. A handsome, intelligent, wealthy young man named Richard Loeb began telling fraternity mates at the Zeta Beta Tau fraternity at the University of Chicago that he knew what the police should do to find information. He suggested that the cops take the time to find the drugstore the Franks had been told to go to the night of the kidnapping. He stated that he had read many detective novels and he knew enough to check on these drugstores on his own. He suggested to the campus liaison for the *Evening*

American, Howard Mayer, that he should go with Loeb and find this drugstore. Mayer decided he would do exactly that, and just as they were about to leave, two *Daily News* reporters entered the fraternity house and agreed to go with them.

They traveled around the city, visiting various drugstores in the city. Eventually, they made their way to the Van de Bogert & Ross Drugstore and, when they went inside to ask the druggist if calls had been received there the night of the kidnapping, their suspicions were confirmed. The druggist admitted that calls for Mr. Franks had been received there the night of the crime. Loeb was ecstatic.

"This is the place!" he reportedly yelled. "This is what comes from reading detective stories."

One of the reporters became curious about Loeb. He asked if Loeb knew the Franks and, in particular, Bobby. Loeb nodded.

"If I were going to murder anybody," he added, with a smile, "I would murder just such a cocky little son of a bitch as Bobby Franks."

The day after this bizarre incident, the body of Bobby Franks was laid out on a cold autopsy table. Dr. Joseph Springer, with the Coroner's Department, performed the grisly task. He concluded that Bobby Franks had died due to suffocation. He guessed that Bobby's killer had either pressed his hand over the boy's mouth and nose or had stuffed something down his throat that suffocated him. He also found numerous other wounds on the body and made the suggestion that the young man had fought his attackers for his life.

The remaining wounds included small lacerations to both side of his head. He also found wounds and bleeding from some sort of blunt object being used against Bobby's forehead. Finally, Springer reached the grim conclusion that some form of sexual molestation had taken place.

The police began to question those who might know the area around Wolf Lake and the culvert where the body had been found. In the course of their investigations, they came across the game warden who had jurisdiction over the Wolf Lake area. He was asked if he had seen anyone around the area on the day and night of the kidnapping and killing. Then he was asked if there was anyone who was a regular to the area who might have seen something as well. It was then that the game warden produced the name Nathan Leopold.

Nathan Leopold was a bit like Mr. Loeb. He was from a wealthy family and was well educated. He liked to bird watch and was often found looking for birds in the Wolf Lake area. The police decided to track down the nineteen-year-old man and ask him some questions. When the police found Nathan, he was agreeable, answered their questions, and provided details about his bird-watching expeditions to the area. His story was convincing and he was released; no charges were pressed against him at that time.

The Leopold family was well-respected in the city of Chicago. They were German Jews who had immigrated to the United States in the 1800s. The family had gotten its wealth transporting grain, minerals, and other materials on Lake Michigan and the other Great Lakes. The Leopold family, along with the Loebs, also lived in the same neighborhood as the Franks.

Two big breaks were about to fall into the investigators' laps. The first was a cab driver who came forward and told police about two young men who had paid him to drive them to the Franks house. Once the two men arrived at the home, they sat in the cab for some time, never leaving the vehicle, and then ordered the driver to take them to another location. He described how the two young men were well dressed and described their clothing.

The next big break came with further investigation of the pair of eyeglasses found. The questioning of the eyeglass manufacturers was about to pay off as someone noticed that the hinges on the glasses were unique. In fact, the hinges were so different that only three pairs of eyeglasses had been sold with those particular hinges. The police quickly asked for a list of those who had purchased glasses with those hinges. Right away, one of the names jumped off the page. The name was Nathan Leopold.

On May 29, 1924, the police decided it was time to question Nathan Leopold once again. However, the State's Attorney was wary of dragging the son of a prominent and wealthy family in handcuffs through the streets to police headquarters. It was decided that Nathan Leopold would be brought to a room at the LaSalle Hotel and questioned.

The police arrived in the afternoon at the Leopold house. They took him to the room and asked him if he had recently lost his eyeglasses in the Wolf Lake area. At first, Leopold stated he had not lost his glasses. As he sat in the room answering questions, police searched the Leopold home where and investigation failed to turn up the glasses.

Leopold looked at the glasses the police had with them and confirmed that they were indeed his. He stated he must have lost them days before Bobby's death when he had been at Wolf Lake bird watching. He indicated he had fallen during that trip and that the glasses must have tumbled from his pocket.

One of the investigators asked Leopold to put the glasses in his pocket and re-enact the fall. Nathan did so, placing them in his breast pocket and attempting, several times, to recreate the fall. The glasses stayed firmly in his pocket. Now the police began to intensify their questions.

Leopold began giving very vague and uncertain answers

to these questions. The police asked him what he had done the day of the kidnapping and murder. Eventually, under the ever-increasing pressure of the questions, he stated he has spent the day with his friend Richard Loeb. He also claimed he and Richard had been eating, drinking, and bird watching in Lincoln Park. Further, he stated that once the two of them had enjoyed dinner together, they had picked up two girls and gone driving until they ended up back at Leopold's home where his aunt and uncle awaited a ride back to their house.

It was like sharks in the water sensing blood and a struggling swimmer available for the police. Leopold was nervous and seemed unsure of details. So, they pressed harder. Leopold seemed to regain his composure and calm himself as the pressure increased, however. He answered calmly, quickly and certainly. The questions began to turn toward his personal life.

The police learned quite a bit about Nathan Leopold. They found out he had graduated from the University of Chicago and had been attending law school. He had plans to go to Harvard Law School later that year. He was good with languages and could speak five fluently with familiarity in fifteen others. He owned a Mammoth Multiplex typewriter and even agreed with the police that his education was enough for him to have composed the ransom note. He also agreed that the note had legal wording but was probably not written by a lawyer. Nathan Leopold's typewriter was quickly confiscated by the police.

Leopold admitted knowing both the Franks family and Bobby in particular. He also stated he knew about the murder and the case surrounding it and had been following it through the media.

Leopold also admitted he had been planning to translate the works of an Italian writer who wrote about various kinds of sexual perversion. However, he denied being a homosexual and denied having had sexual relations with his friend, Richard Loeb.

The questioning went on until four in the morning. At that time, Leopold was allowed to go back to the police station where he would sleep until the next round of questioning. As Nathan Leopold laid down on a hard cot in a cell at that police station, probably believing he had held his own and out-foxed the police, he had no idea that Richard Loeb had also been picked up by the police. He had no idea that Loeb was just down the hall at the LaSalle Hotel at the same time he was undergoing questioning. Most importantly, he had no idea that Loeb's story was vastly different than the one Leopold had just spun for the police.

Richard Loeb had found the police at his door not long after Nathan Leopold had been put into a car and taken to the hotel. His story was that he had been with Leopold throughout the afternoon, but that they had parted at dinnertime. Loeb stated he could not remember what he had done that evening. He was pressed for details, but resolutely stated he could not remember what he had done that night.

That night, and before the questioning could begin again, a mutual friend of Leopold and Loeb managed to speak with Loeb. The message he gave was: "Leopold said to tell the truth about the two girls. Tell the police what you did with them. You can't get in any worse trouble than you are now. He said you'd understand."

The next day, Loeb's story suddenly matched that of Leopold's. The details were fuzzy and he was unable to clarify them and stated the reason for that was that he had been drinking heavily that night and couldn't remember clearly.

Surprisingly, the police bought this line from Loeb. In fact, the State's Attorney took the two boys out for a lavish dinner the next day. Once the dinner was done the two boys even spoke to reporters. "I don't blame the police for holding me," stated Leopold to a reporter from the *Chicago Tribune*, "I was at the culvert the Saturday and Sunday before the glasses were found and it is quite possible I lost my glasses there."

The reporters began to ask around about the two boys. They found that Leopold was part of a law student study group. Other members of this group informed the reporters that they knew Leopold typed up study sheets on a Hammond typewriter but they also knew he owned a portable typewriter. They gave the reporters copies of the study sheets Leopold had typed up with the portable typewriter. They immediately compared the study sheets with the ransom note.

The typing matched perfectly.

Leopold admitted he had typed study sheets using a portable typewriter, but then he denied owning the machine. His house was searched, but no portable typewriter was found. The police then questioned the servants in the house and a maid stated she thought she remembered there being a portable typewriter at one time, but had no idea where it had gone.

Suddenly the police were concerned with Nathan Leopold and Richard Loeb. They were not as worried about the fact that both of them were from prominent families as the State's Attorney was. So, they began digging. They began questioning more servants. They talked to the chauffeur at the Leopold's house. He contradicted Nathan's story about him having the car that evening by stating he had been working on the family car all day long and was certain it had been in the garage in the evening when he went home.

It was a hole in their stories big enough for the police to bring the two men in for questioning again. They kept them in separate rooms and made sure no one visited them. This time there was no sham of being polite or treating the young men as special. The questioning was intense. When Loeb was confronted with the story about the car, he asked what Leopold had told them. When he was informed the information had come from the chauffeur and not Leopold himself, Loeb grew pale and sick and then asked to speak with Crowe. It was then that the real story about what happened to Bobby Franks began to emerge.

Chapter Six
What Happened to Bobby Franks

As the police detectives sat in the room looking at the two boys, they began to realize what had happened, and the shock was something that caught these hardened pros by surprise. These were people who had dealt with gangsters and murderers of all kinds, but nothing like this had ever come across their desks before.

It was a game. Leopold and Loeb were two, young, rich men with time on their hands and a conviction that they were better than anyone else. They had spent hours, days, countless weeks, plotting and talking about committing the "perfect crime." They both felt that their intelligence was so much greater than everyone else's that they could easily commit an act as outrageous as murder, hide the body, and then confound the police and, thus, get away with the crime.

After weeks of working out the plot, the two young men decided on a course of action. They would pick someone to kidnap. They would get the ransom money and get away with it. They would kill their victim immediately after the kidnapping and never have any intention of giving the victim back to their family.

After researching various schemes, the two of them decided it would be best to kidnap someone younger than either of them. They would send a ransom note after kidnapping the victim and have the victim's father go to a drugstore near a train station. They would call that store and tell the victim's father to get on a certain train where the father would then find a note waiting for him that would instruct him to throw the money from the train at a certain point. At that point the two young men would be waiting for the money to fall.

The two of them knew they were going to commit a kidnapping, but they decided that they would pick the victim on the day of the crime. The only requirement they had for their prey was that he would have a wealthy father who could pay the ransom they intended. They also agreed that the victim should be someone they could lure into the car easily. Soon after that, they both knew that the victim would have to die so that there would be no risk of the quarry identifying them later.

On the fateful day that would be the last day of Bobby Franks' life, the two young men got into their car and headed for Harvard School to pick a victim. They would pick at random.

Before they decided on a student, they had briefly considered kidnapping one of their own relatives, or even one of their own fathers. However, they soon dismissed this idea because they knew that they would quickly be prime suspects when someone in their own family ended up murdered.

Once the victim had been killed, they also decided they would have to do something to try and conceal the identity of the victim. And they needed a place to hide the body. Leopold had stumbled across the culvert at Wolf Lake on one of his bird watching expeditions and knew it was hidden enough to be perfect for hiding the corpse. They also figured that the culvert would prevent the need for digging a grave or getting dirt on their clothing or hands.

While sitting in their car on that day, the watched the students come and go from the Harvard School. Several young men had no idea that they had been considered and then dismissed by the two men who thought they were so superior that it was their right to murder someone they felt was inferior to them. Then Richard Loeb saw Bobby Franks and recognized him. Richard also knew that Bobby would come with him easily and probably get right into the car without putting up a fight.

Loeb approached the young man. He knew Bobby had played at the Loeb's tennis courts and had an interest in tennis. So, he walked up to Bobby Franks and told him he had just purchased a new tennis racket. He wondered if Bobby would like to take a look at it. Bobby agreed without any hesitation and walked with the man he knew toward the car and then climbed in.

As soon as Bobby Franks entered the car he was hit on the head with a chisel. Bobby crumpled toward the floor of the car and then a cloth was stuffed down his throat. It was the cloth down his throat that suffocated the boy.

With their victim now either dead or unconscious on the floor of the car, the two young men covered him with a rug and headed towards the Indiana border. Along the way they found a secluded spot and pulled over to the side of the road. Once they had pulled the car over, the two of them got out, uncovered the body, and removed the boy's clothing. They callously tossed the clothing beside the road, climbed back into the car, and drove off again, once again covering the body.

All of their work had made the boys hungry. So, they drove to a hot dog stand in Hammond, Indiana. They ate calmly and then stayed in the Hammond area until the sun started to go down. Once that happened, they both got into the car and headed back home. Along the way they stopped to make the infamous phone call to the Franks' home. Then they stopped to address the envelope with the ransom note in it and mailed it along with the specialized instructions for its delivery.

Leopold and Loeb then headed back to Loeb's house. Once there, they burned the clothes they wore that had bloodstains on them and set to work cleaning up the bloodstains in the rental car. Once they felt they had that taken care of, they entertained themselves by playing casino. They stayed up late into the night playing the game and then, once they had called it a night, they threw out the chisel used to hit Bobby in the head.

They finished their game the next day when they met and decided how they would get the ransom money. They put the kidnap note on the train, in the last car. Leopold then made the call to the Franks' home with the instructions on where to go and which drugstore he needed to be waiting. When Mr. Franks didn't show up at the drugstore, the two boys knew right then that their perfect crime and all of the planning was for nothing.

Once the two boys started talking, they did not stop until the entire sordid tale had been told. It was Loeb who broke first and spilled the story. Once he was done, he looked at the police detectives standing around him who were silently looking at him, piercing him with their stares.

"I just want to say that I offer no excuse, but that I am fully convinced that neither the idea nor the act would have occurred to me had it not been for the suggestion and stimulus of Leopold. Furthermore, I do not believe that I would have been capable of having killed Franks."

With the story in their hands and in their heads, the detectives walked down the hall to where Leopold was sitting, surrounded by his own detectives. Once they laid out the confession Loeb had just given them, Leopold confessed as well. When the detectives looked at the two statements they saw that they were almost identical except for some very curious differences.

Leopold's confession stated that Loeb had done the actual act of killing Bobby Franks. At the same time, of course, Loeb had stated Leopold had done the act. When the press got hold of the two stories, they decided to side with Loeb. They began to portray Leopold as a kind of mad and evil genius who had dominated and controlled his friend with his vast intellect.

The police, on the other hand, had no desire to portray one over the other in any particular way. They just knew that they had a dead boy and that these two were responsible in one way or another. Both of them were charged with premeditated murder and kidnapping.

With the final charges and the revelation that the two killers were also young men set the stage for the entrance of one of the most colorful figures in the history of the legal profession in American history. It was time for Clarence Darrow to come into the picture.

Chapter Seven
The Lawyer

Clarence Darrow was not, at that time, known for his criminal defense skills. He was known as an ardent opponent of the death penalty. He was known for his wit and his intelligence. He was known as a man with immense talent, but he had no idea that the biggest case in the country, at that time, was about to fall right into his lap.

The tale of Leopold and Loeb was everywhere and it seemed that everyone wanted to know everything about the case. The public was shocked by the details of the murder. They were calling for blood and they wanted the two young men who were accused and had confessed to this crime to hang as soon as possible.

The local Chicago newspapers declared that a crime of this nature had never before been seen in this city which was already famous for crimes and criminals. The *Chicago Tribune* printed a lengthy editorial describing the case.

> "In view of the fact that the solving of the Franks kidnapping and death bring to notice a crime that is unique in Chicago's annals, and perhaps unprecedented in American criminal history, the *Tribune* this morning gives to the report of the case many columns of space for news, comment and pictures.
> "The diabolical spirit evinced in the planned kidnapping and murder; the wealth and prominence of the families whose sons are involved; the highest mental attainments of the youths, the suggestions of perversion; the strange quirks indicated in the confession that the child was slain for a ransom, for experience, for the satisfaction of a desire for 'deep plotting,' combined to put the case in a class by itself."

The pain and anguish seemed to be particularly acute in

Chicago's Jewish community. It was unthinkable that such a horrendous crime had been committed by two of their own and by two young men who were part of the Jewish social elite. The two young men had everything at their feet and within reach of their fingers. They had money, education, and a life of privilege, and that they had used that to do something like this shook the community to its core. Albert Loeb was a wealthy man who ran Sears and Roebuck's catalog business. Nathan Leopold, Sr. had made his money in the shipping business. Both of them were respected.

The only thing that the Jewish community seemed to find some comfort in the entire incident was that the two Jewish men had also killed another Jew. If the victim had not been Jewish, it was feared the backlash against the Jewish community would be so great that it wouldn't be able to recover.

Meanwhile, within the police department, the confessions had been taken and the investigation moved forward. The investigators started searching for more evidence. A clerk was found who identified Leopold as the man who had purchased a bottle of hydrochloric acid. Leopold then described how he had used the acid to pour on Bobby Frank's face, hands, and genitals.

Then Crowe took the two accused men on a search for further evidence. They found the chisel that had been used to knock Bobby out. Then they found the clothes that had been thrown on the side of the road. Eventually, they also found Bobby's shoes. In short, they had enough evidence that things looked pretty cut and dried as far as the District Attorney was concerned.

Jacob Loeb, the uncle of Richard, attempted to get in touch with the two boys, but he was not told where they were. He knew that they would need a lawyer. So, Jacob Loeb visited the apartment of one of the most famous and prominent attorneys in not only the city of Chicago, but the entire country, Clarence Darrow. He begged the man to take the case.

"Get them a life sentence instead of death," he begged. "That's all we ask. We'll pay anything, only for God's sake, don't let them hang."

Darrow had long been known for his anti-death penalty stance. So, he decided to take the case, but not for the fee or any of the money the Loeb family promised. He saw the attention this case was already getting. It would be a national forum for him to present his reasons for being against capital punishment.

The problem was that Darrow was battling uphill from the start. Leopold and Loeb had already damaged their own case by giving, writing, and signing their confessions. Then they had helped the police find the evidence to be used against them. They had also not shut up while in captivity, but had continued to talk and blab to the police, reporters, and anyone else who wanted to listen to them.

In fact, Leopold had confessed the premeditative nature of the crime to a reporter before his uncle approached Darrow. "Why, we even rehearsed the kidnapping at least three times, carrying it through in all details, lacking only the boy we were to kidnap and kill... It was just an experiment. It is as easy for us to justify as an entomologist in impaling a beetle on a pin."

Meanwhile, also unable to shut up, Loeb was talking to a police captain by saying, "This thing will be the making of me. I'll spend a few years in jail and I'll be released. I'll come out to a new life."

As they talked, the police detectives and reporters took copious, detailed and careful notes. As the files within the police department grew on the two boys, the stories in the papers kept coming out detailing everything they were saying. Still they kept talking.

On Sunday June 1, Clarence Darrow stood with Jacob Loeb at the station until the boys returned with their police escorts from another expedition gathering evidence. Darrow and the other men with him demanded to see them but they were all refused. The District Attorney, Crowe, had already lined up three forensic psychiatrists (also known as "alienists") to talk to the boys that afternoon. They were to talk to the two men and determine that they were sane in addition to being guilty.

Darrow and the two men with him turned away and left. However, Darrow was back at Crowe's office the very next morning. He again demanded to speak to Leopold and Loeb. Once again, Crowe tried to deny him the opportunity, because he wanted his alienists to spend more time with the two young men and gather more evidence of their sanity and guilt. Crowe was just assuming that Darrow had plans to plead the two boys as not guilty by reason of insanity, and he wanted an airtight case to cut Darrow off from that course of action.

Darrow had been busy the evening before. He had contacted Judge John R. Caverly and received a signed order that allowed him to meet with his clients before they were confined to the county jail. Crowe was beaten and the meeting between Darrow and the two men was arranged.

"Be polite. Be courteous," he instructed the two men. "But don't give Crowe any more help. Just keep quiet and refuse to answer any questions."

Meanwhile, life in jail was not exactly that hard for the two privileged boys. In fact, they were being as pampered in jail as they were throughout their lives. Stein's Restaurant was busy catering to their every need when it came to food. They were also provided with cigarettes and as much booze as they wanted. Of course, it was Prohibition but it was sneaked to them anyway.

A grand jury was convened on June 5, 1924, and Nathan Leopold and Richard Loeb were indicted on eleven counts of murder and sixteen counts of kidnapping. Twenty-four hours after they were indicted, their full confessions were printed in the newspapers. This combined with rumors that the two boys were going to pay Clarence Darrow a million dollars to keep them from the hangman, fanned the flames of the public and caused an uproar in the community.

Darrow sat down with the two families and wrote a statement for the public and the press. It said, "There will be no large sums of money spent, either for legal or medical talent."

Meanwhile, three top psychiatric experts were brought in from the American Psychiatric Association's annual convention. Dr. William A. White, Dr. William Healy, and Dr. Bernard Glueck were brought on to the defense team. These three men were confirmed Freudian psychiatrists with firm beliefs in the subconscious and compulsions. The team also found two more psychiatrists, Dr. Harold Hulbert and Dr. Carl Bowman.

Leopold in particular was fond of talking to the alienists and psychiatrists. It made him the center of attention and stoked his ego. The sessions also gave him a chance to talk about his favorite topic, himself. His friend Loeb, meanwhile, found the sessions boring and sometimes fell asleep. In either case, neither of the two young men expressed any remorse or regret about what they had done. They were only sad that they had been caught and that they had brought attention and shame on their families.

On July 21, 1924, the trial that the entire country was waiting for began. The press and the city of Chicago were on the edge of their collective seats to hear what Darrow would say. The belief was that he would try to convince the jury that his two clients were insane, but the confessions and their demeanor seemed to contradict this defense. Most of the city, in fact most of the country, wanted to see the two young men hanged.

Chapter Eight
The Trial Starts

The trial began and the world waited in anticipation for what Clarence Darrow would do. Once again, everyone expected him, from the first day, to bring up the suggestion of "not guilty by reason of insanity." Darrow was shrewd and he was smart, and he immediately took the legs out from under the prosecution.

Darrow walked out in front of the judge and the courtroom. He started pleasantly, quietly, in a low voice and assured the court that he would not waste their time and ask for a change of venue. He also said he was not going to waste the court's time by filing motions to separate the two men into two separate trials. He also said he would not be trying to separate the charges into trials for murder and kidnapping. Then, while the prosecution was puzzled and scratching its head, he went in for the kill.

"We want to state frankly here that no one in this case believes that these defendants should be released or are competent to be. We believe that they should be permanently isolated from society. After long reflection and thorough discussion, we have determined to make a motion in this court for each of the defendants in each of the cases to withdraw our pleas of not guilty and enter a plea of guilty."

The courtroom was thunderstruck. With those few words, the prosecution's case and method of attack had been taken away. Plus, with the plea of guilty, Darrow had taken the public out of the mix. Now, there would be no jury, just a judge. Now, he would not have to try to portray the defendants as sympathetic in front of people out for their blood.

Darrow had explained his rationale to the families of the two boys. He had not, however, explained his plan of attack to his two clients until the morning of their court appearance.

"Crowe had you indicted both for murder and for kidnapping," he explained to them. "He'd try you on one charge, say, the murder. If he got less than a hanging verdict, he could turn around and try you on the other charge. There is only one way to deprive him of that second chance—to plead guilty to both charges before he has an opportunity to withdraw one of them. That's why the element of surprise is absolutely necessary."

Darrow was actually trying to play mind games with the judge. He knew that a group of people might easily agree to hang the two young men. With this method, he now placed their fates directly on the head of one man. Darrow felt his odds were better at convincing that one man to spare the boys' lives than he did convincing twelve.

Caverly, the judge, was just as shocked as everyone else. He looked at the two defendants and asked them to approach the bench. He began questioning them by asking, "If your plea be guilty, and the plea of guilty is entered into this case, the court may sentence you to death; the court may sentence you to the penitentiary for the term of your natural life; the court may sentence you to the penitentiary for a term of years not less than fourteen. Now, realizing the consequences of your plea, do you still desire to plead guilty?"

The two young men stood before the judge and a silent courtroom and both nodded and said, "Yes." At the same time the look on their faces seemed to indicate that they were now starting to grasp the full magnitude of the crimes they had committed and the punishments they were facing.

Across the bench from the two boys, the judge's face also showed emotion. Caverly was not a stupid man. He knew and was beginning to understand the full magnitude of the decision that was facing him. He also began to understand the predicament Darrow had just put him in.

At the same time, Judge Caverly was not a weak man. He was sixty-three years old at the time of the trial. He was from an immigrant family, and worked his way up through law school. He supported himself by working in the steel mills. He was coming close to the end of this career on the bench when this trial fell into his lap, and during his career presiding over a courtroom, he had imposed the death penalty five times, but each time had been at the recommendation of a jury.

As Caverly sat back in the seat behind his podium, the State's Attorney, Robert E. Crowe, stepped out from behind his desk and began to deliver his opening statement. He was no longer ruffled from the surprise move Darrow had made. He was calm as he began to speak.

"The evidence in this case will show that Nathan Leopold, Jr. is a young man nineteen years old, that the other defendant, Richard Loeb, is a young man of nineteen years; that they are both sons of highly respected and prominent citizens of this community; that their parents gave them every advantage wealth and indulgence could give to boys. They have attended the best schools in this community and have, from time to time, had private tutors. These young men behaved as a majority of young men in their social set behaved, with the exception that they developed a desire to gamble, and gambled for large stakes, the size of the stakes being such that even their wealthy companions could not sit with them.

"The evidence will further show that along in October or November of last year these two defendants entered into a conspiracy, and in order to gain it they were ready and willing to commit a cold-blooded murder."

Crowe continued to talk. He spoke for nearly an hour. He

laid out the case as he saw it and informed the court of what the State would present to show the guilt of the two young men. Then, an hour later, he summed up by saying, "In the name of the people of the State of Illinois, in the name of the womanhood and the fatherhood, and in the name of the children of the State of Illinois, we are going to demand the death penalty for both of these cold-blooded, cruel, and vicious murderers."

Darrow was given time to respond to the prosecution at this time. He rose again and stepped out into the courtroom and spoke.

"We shall insist in this case, Your Honor," he said, "that, terrible as this is, terrible as any killing is, it would be without precedent if the two boys of this age should be hanged by the neck until dead, and it would in no way bring back Robert Franks or add to the peace and security of this community."

With that out of the way, the case began in earnest. The prosecution started to present witnesses. They began to present gruesome details of the crime. It became obvious that the prosecutors were going to try and present the horror of the crime to the point that the public and the judge would have no choice but to give the death penalty. The defense asked barely any questions to avoid stressing any of the brutal themes given out during the prosecution's case.

Meanwhile, Darrow had his hands full with his two clients. Leopold and Loeb, while appearing to grasp the serious nature of their situation at first, soon lapsed into their old ways. They began talking to reporters again. More distressingly, they began making jokes and acting more like they were at a ball game than fighting for their lives.

The very next day, after the opening statements, Loeb stood in front of the doors of the courtroom and spoke to reporters. He stated he had a very important statement to make and then said, "We are united in one great and profound hope for today. Mr. Leopold and I have gone over the matter and have come to a mutual decision. We have just one hope: that it will be a damned sight cooler than it was yesterday." He then burst into laughter.

Crowe took a week and presented eighty-one witnesses. There was little doubt in anyone's mind that he had proven the two young men's guilt beyond all reason. He rested his case after a week, convinced he had done his job. Of course, at the same time, since the boy's had already pleaded guilty, it was a relatively moot effort.

It was now time for Darrow to take the stage. His plan was to use the forensic psychiatrists, or alienists, to take on the death penalty itself. The entire country, if not the world, was watching and he had the huge stage he had always wanted to take on this cause he felt so deeply about. So, with his doctor's at the ready, Darrow began to present his case.

Chapter Nine
Alienists

Darrow intended to use his forensic psychiatrists, or alienists, to explain that Leopold and Loeb had no choice in their behavior. It was hoped that this would give them a sentence of life in prison, and save them from the hangman's noose.

His two doctors, Hulbert and Bowman, started their investigation by trying to learn everything they could about the two young men. They asked them questions about their lives. They studied every detail about how they had been raised, their behaviors, their dreams, their ambitions. It was initially started to determine if the insanity defense would even be a potential option and, even more importantly, some kind of explanation for why the two of them killed Bobby Franks.

As for Richard Loeb, the two doctors soon discovered, he had a tendency toward crime from a very early age. In fact, his first crimes started at the age of eight or nine. It was then that Richard stole money and other small objects with, according to the report, "absolutely no compunction of guilt or fear connected with this theft...but felt ashamed [when] his lack of skill caused him to be caught."

Loeb continued to steal. The thing was, he was doing it because he enjoyed it and because he wanted to get better at it, not necessarily because of some desire for the object he was stealing. Throughout his years as a teenager, he continued to shoplift.

Like others who become addicted to things that are potentially unhealthy for him, the small thefts were soon not enough to satisfy him. He began to vandalize cars and that soon lead to stealing them. He then started to make harassing phone calls to his school teachers, and that lead to calling the fire department and making false reports. His calls to the fire department soon slid into actually setting fires. Before too long, he was creating them with Nathan Leopold and the two of them became fire for each other.

In 1923, the two young men had decided to plan a burglary. Their intended target was a friend's home while the family was away. To commit the crime, they took a revolver with them in order to shoot the night watchman. They also planned to tie up the maid and took rope with them. On the way to the crime, their car broke down and they aborted their plots to burglarize the home. Instead, they burglarized the Zeta Beta Tau fraternity home that Loeb belonged to in Ann Arbor, Michigan.

When the report of the two doctors was written, it was somehow leaked to the press. On Monday, July 26, the report was published all over the country.

The defense opened their arguments by calling a Dr. William Alanson White who was the head of the St. Elizabeth's Hospital in Washington. The prosecutor, Mr. Crowe, objected and stated: "You do not take a microscope and look into a murder's head to see what state of mind he was in, because if he is insane, he is not responsible, and if he is sane, he is responsible. You look not to his mental condition, but to the facts surrounding the case—did he kill the man because the man debauched his wife? If so, then there is mitigation here...But here is cold-blooded murder, without a defense in fact, and the attempt on a plea of guilty to introduce an insanity defense before your honor is unprecedented. The statute says that is a matter that must be tried by a jury."

Darrow was, once again, cool under the pressure exerted

by the prosecution and stated, "The statute in this state provides that the court may listen to anything, either in the mitigation of the penalty or in aggravation."

In truth, Darrow was playing with semantics. There had never been a precedent for what he was about to do in the state, nor was there really much precedent for this kind of case at all. As such, after this, days of arguing and legal wrangling on both sides occurred.

Once this had been settled, Darrow began to settle into his case. More importantly he began to state his case, and sketch out his defense. He started by making a statement to the court which showed some of Darrow's skill and helped provide ammunition for those who wanted to put him at the top of the legal ladder in the United States.

"Now," he began, "I understand that when everything has been said in this case from the beginning to end, the position of the state's attorney is that the universe will crumble unless these boys are hanged. I must say that I have never before seen the same passion and enthusiasm for the death penalty as I have in this case and there have been thousands of killings before this, much more horrible in details... There have been thousands before, and there will probably be thousands again, whether these boys are hanged or go to prison. If I thought that hanging them would prevent any future murders, I would probably be in favor of doing it. But I have no such feeling.

"What is a mitigating circumstance? Is it youth? If so, why? Simply because the child has not the judgment of life that a grown person has.

"Here are two boys who are minors. The law would forbid them making contracts, forbid them marrying without the consent of their parents, would not permit them to vote. Why? Because they haven't the judgment which only comes with years, because they are not fully responsible.

"I cannot understand the glib, lighthearted carelessness of lawyers who talk of hanging two boys as if they were talking of a holiday or visiting the races."

Documents show Darrow paused here. Newspapers reported that he turned to look at Judge Caverly and that his voice grew hushed in a form of respect.

"I don't believe there is a judge in Cook County that would not take into consideration the mental status of any man before they sentence him to death."

With that, Darrow was done making his case for admission of his alienists. He had stated his case baldly and carefully. He also managed to convince the judge who agreed to hear the evidence of mitigation. Darrow would be allowed to call his alienists, and the report that had been leaked to the press and read by almost everyone, could be read into the court documents. It was a huge key victory for the defense.

Now, it was time for the defense to start presenting the information about how Leopold and Loeb had been raised. It was time to focus on how that had lead them into the life they had lead. It was time to try and convince a judge that the two men, working together, had created a scenario where the only outcome was the terrible death of Bobby Franks. With this, Darrow hoped to save both of them from the hangman's noose.

Chapter Ten
Testifying

As far as Richard Loeb's father, the alienists wrote that they found him to be "fair and just. He is opposed to the boys' drinking and often spoke of it; he is not strict, although the boys may have thought he was. He never used corporal punishment. In early childhood, he was not a play-fellow with the boys...Dick and his brothers loved and worshipped their father and did not want to lose their father's love and respect."

As far as Richard's mother, they knew from talking with him that she was a Catholic woman from a very large family. Her family was not in approval of her marriage to Albert, who was Jewish—this despite his incredible wealth and success. She and Albert had managed to produce four sons: Allan, Ernest, Richard, and Thomas. One of the alienists labeled Ann Bohnen Loeb as "poised, keen, alert, and interested."

Huge sections of the report show that Richard Loeb exhibited what could only be called psychotic characteristics. Despite this, there were also instances within his life where he showed a much softer side of himself. For example, there was once a time when Richard witnessed an auto accident. In fact, Richard had been driving, and had collided with a horse and buggy. It was entirely an accident, nothing he could have avoided, and he realized a woman and her son had been involved and that the son was injured. Dick took the mother and child to a hospital and, once he arrived there, realized the woman was also injured. At the sight of her injuries he wept and nearly fainted. He then returned to the hospital every day, bringing flowers, fruit, and the best food. He also persuaded his father to pay for her hospital bill and then to pay off a mortgage on the woman's home. He convinced his father to pay to send her on a trip during the winter to help her recover from the ordeal as well.

When Richard was four, a woman named Struthers became his governess. She was Canadian and was very devoted to him, in particular; she was keen to educate Richard. She provided coaching, tutoring, and encouragement. Richard was showing signs of being extremely bright, already testing at an IQ level of 160. Thanks to the teaching of Struthers, Richard accelerated through school and finished grade school by the age of twelve and was done with high school by fourteen. At that same age, he went to the University of Chicago. Not long after that, after an argument with Richard's mother, the Struthers woman left the Loeb home.

One of the alienists found and interviewed Miss Struthers and wrote that she was, "too anxious to have him become an ideal boy. She would not overlook some of his faults and was too quick in her punishment and therefore he built up the habit of lying without compunction and with increasing skill. She was quite unaware of the fact that he had become a petty thief and a play detective."

Soon after entering the University, Richard decided he needed time away from his family. He enrolled in the University of Michigan and soon became one of the youngest graduates of that University at the age of seventeen. His grades were not spectacular, as life away from home seemed to activate some sloth in him, and he was lazy and unmotivated.

When it came to the subject of sex, Richard had no education. His age, and the fact that Miss Struthers had not spent any time discussing the topic, made him stunted on this topic. He had, in fact, little interest in sex, and what little about it he knew, he got through conversations with the family chauffeur. He believed that he was less sexually potent that any of his friends and, despite his looks and ample opportunity; he did not participate as much as some of his friends. He did take advantage from time to time, but it was not something he pursued with any passion or interest. He had no long-term relationships during high school or college with women.

Although Loeb had no need for women and no skill with them, he developed immense skill with lying. In fact, he needed it to continue his career in crime. Although he admitted to the alienists who interviewed him that he knew lying was wrong, he felt no guilt about it in the least. As his crimes grew, he began to fancy himself some kind of criminal mastermind. It was then that he began to develop the idea of pulling off one great crime and then quit. This was the first germ of an idea that would lead to the death of Bobby Franks.

Dr. White spoke in open court and summarized his findings and feelings about Richard Loeb. He said, "All of Dickie's life, from the beginning of his antisocial activities, has been in the direction of his own self-destruction. He himself has definitely and seriously considered suicide. He told me that he was satisfied with his life and that so far as he could see, life had nothing more to offer, because he had run the gamut. He was at the end of the situation. He has lived his life out."

White then went on to testify that he felt the major facet of Richard's personality was infantilism. He also stated he felt that Richard was the most likely candidate for having done the actual killing of Bobby Franks.

Up next was Dr. Healy and his assessment of Richard Loeb. It soon became obvious that Healy did not think very much of the young man at all. He said, "To my mind the crime itself is the direct result of diseased motivation of Loeb's mental life. The planning and commission was only possible because he was abnormal mentally, with pathological split personality."

The next doctor to discuss Richard Loeb was Dr. Glueck. Glueck was intrigued by Loeb's personality and stated, "I was amazed at the absolute absence of any signs of normal feelings, such as one would expect under the circumstances. He showed no remorse, no regret, no compassion for the people involved in this situation...He told me the details of the crime, including the fact that he struck the blow."

According to the testimony records, Dr. Glueck's was the most revealing when it came to discussing who had actually committed the murder. There was another boy to discuss, however, and the alienists had opinions about him as well.

Of the two boys, Nathan Leopold was the one that the alienists seemed to find the biggest connection to, and held the most sympathy for. He was the youngest of his siblings, with three older brothers and he had been given the nickname of Babe by his family. When he was young, he had been in bed much of the time, too sickly to wander outside and play with friends and he suffered a number of glandular problems. So sick was he that doctors told him and his parents that they doubted he would live to the age he had so far.

Nathan's mother died when he was seventeen from nephritis. She had been ill, much like he was, ever since his birth. Nathan had been informed repeatedly that the reason his mother was sick was because of him and this created a terrific guilt inside him. Once she died, an aunt named Birdie Schwab came in and managed the Leopold household.

Much like his friend, Richard Loeb, Nathan Leopold was scarily intelligent. In fact, he was a certified genius with an IQ of 210. According to his family, he spoke his first words at four months.

Nathan had several governesses, but they always had to divide their time between the four boys. Birdie and the governesses were the ones charged with raising the boys as Nathan's father, Nathan Leopold, Sr. was too busy being a businessman to spend much time with his children.

Nathan's intelligence soon became a problem for him when he was at school. His brain gave him a feeling of superiority over his classmates and this made him exceedingly unpopular. He soon began to attend the Harvard School, but the teasing from his classmates began in earnest there. He had few, if any, friends and was not popular in the least, as he was perceived as conceited and arrogant.

At the age of sixteen, he attended the University of Chicago just as his friend Richard Loeb had. By this time, he and Loeb had already formed a friendship and when Loeb transferred to the University of Michigan, Nathan followed. When he got there, he found that he and Loeb were not able to spend as much time together because Loeb was part of a fraternity and Nathan was not. In fact, Richard Loeb had been admitted into the Zeta Beta Tau house under the provision that he not spend time with Nathan Leopold. Rumors had begun to circulate that the two were involved in a homosexual relationship and the fraternity wanted to dispel those rumors. After a time, Nathan returned to the University of Chicago and graduated Phi Betta Kappa and then began law school.

When it came to women, Nathan had no abilities at all. The only relationships he had with women were with prostitutes. In fact, he confessed to the alienists that he was not attracted, or interested, in women; he stated that he found them inferior to him intellectually.

Nathan Leopold had become an atheist after the death of his mother. Once that happened, his world was turned upside down. He could not believe that God would exist in a world that allowed such a thing to occur.

As they interviewed Nathan Leopold, all of the alienists stated they felt he was honest, straight-forward, and very frank. Unlike Richard Loeb, whom they felt lied as easily as most people sneezed, they felt Leopold was as truthful as could be.

The reported stated, "The patient makes no effort to shift the blame for the crime to his companion, although he insists that he did not desire to commit the crime and derived no special pleasure from it. He feels that his only reason for going into it was his pact of friendship with his companion, and his companion's desire to do it. Since he had a marked sex drive, and has not been able to satisfy it in the normal heterosexual relations, this has undoubtedly been a profound upsetting condition on his whole emotional life. He endeavored to compensate for his physical inferiority by a world of fantasy in which his desire for physical perfection could be satisfied. We see him therefore fantasizing himself as a slave, who is the strongest man in the world. In some way or other within these fantasies he saved the life of the king. The king was grateful and wanted to give him his liberty but the slave refused."

These slave fantasies, Leopold claimed to have had since the ages of four or five. He continued to have them throughout his younger days and into his teenage years.

As Leopold continued to speak with the alienists, he found that he enjoyed discussing his life-philosophies. These were discussed in the report as, "In such a philosophy, without any place for emotions and feelings, the intelligence reigns supreme. The only crime that he can commit is a crime of intelligence, a mistake of intelligence, and for that he is fully responsible. In the scheme of the perfect man which he drew up, he gave Dickie a scoring of 90, himself a scoring of 63, and various other of their mutual acquaintances various marks ranging from 30 to 40."

It was Dr. White who looked at Leopold through the prism of the Franks murder and then at Nathan's abnormal fantasy life and personalities. He stated, within the report, "Dickie needed an audience. In his fantasies the criminalistic gang was his audience. In reality, Babe was his audience and Babe's tendencies could be expressed—as they were in the king-slave fantasy—as a constant swing between a feeling of physical inferiority and one of intellectual superiority. Leopold is the slave who makes Dickie the king, maintains him in his kingdom. I cannot see how Babe would have entered into it at all alone because he had no criminalistic tendencies in any sense as Dickie did, and I don't think Dickie would have ever functioned to this extend all by himself. So these two boys, with their peculiarly inter-digited personalities, came into this emotional compact with the Franks homicide as a result."

Another of the alienists also saw this co-dependent connection between the two boys. Dr. Healy stated, "Leopold was to have the privilege of inserting his penis between Loeb's legs at special dates. At one time it was to be three times in two months—if they continued their criminalistic activities together."

Healy felt that Leopold's personality was completely paranoid. Healy quoted a statement Leopold made that was particularly chilling in which he said, "making up my mind whether or not to commit murder was practically the same as making up my mind whether or not I should eat pie for supper, whether it would give me pleasure or not."

Dr. Glueck was also chilled by concept Nathan Leopold had derived from Nietzche. Leopold became enamored of the concept of the Superman. This was a concept shared by Loeb and the combined fascination with this concept added to the brew that erupted in murder. According to Glueck, "I think the Franks crime was perhaps the inevitable outcome of this curious coming together of two pathologically disordered personal ties, each one of whom brought into the relationship a phase of their personality which made their contemplation and the execution of this crime possible."

The prosecutor decided to probe this further with Glueck. He asked if he could determine a motivation for the murder. Glueck responded, "I don't know that there was a direct motive for this crime. I do feel that Loeb had in his mind probably the motive of complete power, potency, the realization of the fantasy of a perfect crime."

"How about Leopold?" asked Crowe.

"I don't know that he had any," Glueck responded with a shrug.

With that, the alienists' testimony ended. It was time for Clarence Darrow to take center-stage once again and give his final summation. He was pleading for their lives.

Chapter Eleven
Darrow Closes it Out

Clarence Darrow began his summation on August 22, 1924. The entire speech lasted two hours. Not all of this speech is quoted here, but it is widely considered to be the best he ever gave, throughout his career.

To start off, he stated that, "never had there been a case in Chicago, where on a plea of guilty a boy under twenty-one had been sentenced to death. I will raise that age and say, never has there been a case where a human being under the age of twenty-three has been sentenced to death. Why need the state's attorney ask for something that never before has been demanded?"

With that, he continued, facing the rest of the court and speaking calmly and confidently to the judge. "I know that in the last ten years four hundred and fifty people have been indicted for murder in the city of Chicago and have pleaded guilty. Only one has been hanged. And my friend who is prosecuting this case deserves the honor of that hanging while he was on the bench. But his 'victim' was forty years old."

Darrow began to attack the prosecutions case and even began picking apart the phrases the prosecution had used throughout the trial. In particular, he did not appreciate the use of the term "cold-blooded murder."

"They call it a cold-blooded murder because they want to take human lives," he said, "This is the most cold-blooded murder, says the State, that ever occurred. I have never yet tried a case where the state's attorney did not say that it was the most cold-blooded, inexcusable, premeditated case that ever occurred. If it was murder, there never was such a murder. Lawyers are apt to say that.

"I insist, Your Honor, that under all fair rules and measurements, this was one of the lease dastardly and cruel of any that I have seen. Poor little Bobby Franks suffered very little. It was all over in fifteen minutes after he got into the car, and he probably never knew it or thought of it. That does not justify it, but it is done.

"This is a senseless, useless, purposeless, motiveless act of two boys. There was not a particle of hate, there was not a gain of malice, there was no opportunity to be cruel except as death is cruel—and death is cruel."

Darrow then turned his attention to the prosecution's assertion that the entire crime had been an attempt to gain money. The prosecution had insisted that the ransom was the real motivation, and Darrow dismissed this as ridiculous. He pointed out that Loeb alone had $3,000 in his checking account at the time of the crime. Leopold's father was just about to give him that very same amount of money for a trip to Europe that he had planned. Obviously, stated Darrow, money was not the motivation here.

"It would be trifling, excepting, Your Honor, that we are dealing in human life. And we are dealing in more than that; we are dealing in the future fate of two families," he stated when discussing the assertion that the two young men had amassed a huge gambling debt. In fact, the debt owed was $90.

"We are talking of placing a blot upon the escutcheon of two houses that do not deserve it. And all that the State can get out of their imagination is that there was a game of bridge and one lost ninety dollars to the other, and therefore they went out and committed murder."

It was now time for Darrow to discuss the mental state of

his two clients. He was to use some of the material discussed by the alienists.

"They had a weird, almost impossible relationship. Leopold, with his obsession of the superman, had repeatedly said that Loeb was his idea of the superman. He had the attitude toward him that one has to his most devoted friend, or that a man has to a lover. Without the combination of these two, nothing of this sort probably would have happened. All the testimony of the alienists shows that this terrible act was the act of immature and diseased brains, the act of children.

"Nobody can explain it any other way. No one can imagine it any other way. It is not possible that it could have happened in any other way."

Darrow was near the end of his speech now. He had been talking for nearly two hours and it was time to make his final, last plea for the lives of these two young murderers. He paused and then began speaking again.

"I do not know how much salvage there is in these two boys. I hate to say it in their presence, but what is there to look forward to? I do not know but that Your Honor would be merciful if you tied a rope around their necks and let them die; merciful to them, but not merciful to civilization, and not merciful to those who would be left behind. To spend the balance of their lives in prison is mighty little to look forward to, if anything. So far as I am concerned, it is over. And I think here of the stanza of Houseman:

"'Now hollow fires burn out to black, and lights are fluttering low, square your shoulders, lift your pack, and leave your friends and go. O never fear, lads, naught's to dread. Look not left nor right. In all the endless road you tread, there's nothing but the night'

"I care not, Your Honor, whether the march begins at the

gallows or when the gates of Joliet close upon them, there is nothing but the night, and that is little for any human being to expect.

"None of are unmindful of the public; courts are not, and juries are not. We placed our fate in the hands of a trained court, thinking that he would be more mindful and considerate than a jury. I cannot say how people feel. I have stood here for three months as one might stand at the ocean trying to sweep back the tide. I hope the seas are subsiding and the wind is falling, and I believe they are, but I wish to make no false pretense to this court.

"The easy thing and the popular thing to do is hang my clients. I know it. Men are women who do not think will applaud. The cruel and thoughtless will approve. It will be easy today; but in Chicago, and reaching out over the length and breadth of the land, more and more fathers and mothers, the humane, the kind and the hopeful, who are gaining an understanding and asking questions not only about these poor boys, but their own—these will join in no acclaim at the death of my clients. They would ask that the shedding of blood be stopped, and that the normal feelings of man resume their sway. And as the days and the months and the years go on, they will ask it more and more.

"But, Your Honor, what they shall ask may not count. I know the easy way. I know Your Honor stands between the future and the present. I know the future is with me, and what I stand for here; not merely for the lives of these two unfortunate lads, but for all boys and girls; for all of the young, and as far as possible, for all of the old. I am pleading for life, understanding, charity, kindness, and the infinite mercy that considers all. I am pleading that we overcome cruelty with kindness, and hatred with love. I know the future is on my side.

"I feel that I should apologize for the length of time I have taken. This case may not be as important as I think it is, and I am sure I do not need to tell this court, or to tell my friends that I would fight just as hard for the poor as for the rich. If I should succeed in saving these boys' lives and do nothing for the progress of the law, I should feel sad, indeed. If I can succeed, my greatest reward and my greatest hope will be that I have done something for the tens of thousands of other boys, for the countless unfortunates who must tread the same road in blind childhood that these boys have trod; that I have done something to help human understanding, to tempter justice with mercy, to overcome hate with love."

With those words, Clarence Darrow finished. Silence filled the courtroom. He sat down and the prosecution took its turn. They managed to take two whole days to close their case.

Eventually, the judge retired to his chambers to decide a sentence. On September 19, 1924, Judge Caverly returned to the courtroom and announced his decision.

He started off my confirming that he felt that the insanity defense was not applicable for this particular case. At the same time he acknowledged that, "they have been shown in essential respects to be abnormal; had they been normal they would not have committed the crime." He then went on to praise the work of the various alienists and stated he felt their work and reports would provide invaluable assistance to cases and studies done on criminals in the future.

"The testimony in this case reveals a crime of singular atrocity," he stated. "It is in a sense inexplicable; but it is not thereby rendered less inhuman or repulsive."

He paused at this point to explain to the courtroom the various meanings of murder and kidnapping. He also explained the potential punishments for both of those crimes. Finally, after this legal dissertation, he arrived at his sentencing.

"It would have been the path of least resistance to impose the extreme penalty of the law. In choosing imprisonment instead of death, the court is moved chiefly by the consideration of the age of the defendants. Life imprisonment may not, at the moment, strike the public imagination as forcibly as would death by hanging; but to the offenders, particularly of the type they are, the prolonged suffering of years of confinement may well be the severer form of retribution and expiation.

"For the crime of murder, confinement at the penitentiary at Joliet for the term of their natural lives.

"For the crime of kidnapping for ransom, similar confinement for the term of ninety-nine years."

He also asked that the authorities never seek to parole either of the two men. With that, the sentences were written and Richard Loeb and Nathan Leopold were carted off to Joliet penitentiary.

Chapter Twelve
The Aftermath

Not a single person involved in this crime and the subsequent trial was ever the same after the trial was concluded. Judge Caverly, for example, checked himself, along with his wife, into a hospital immediately after he read the sentences. He claimed it was due to the extreme strain and sheer exhaustion he was experiencing after the trial. Once he felt he was well enough to recover, he returned to the bench but insisted on only hearing divorce cases.

He told reporters, "My health has been sapped."

The father of Bobby Franks, Jacob, came out after the sentencing and told the reporters that he had reversed his initial call for the hanging of the two boys. "My wife and I never believed Nathan, Jr., and Richard should be hanged."

According to reports, he was never the same after the death of Bobby. His health declined and he died only a few years after the end of the trial. Bobby's mother, Flora, was reported delusional and suffered numerous breakdowns after his body was found and during the trial. She eventually recovered enough to remarry.

Albert Loeb was already bedridden due to a severe heart attack before his son committed the crime for which he was sentenced. He spent the entire time of the trial just trying to stay alive. He only managed to live an additional month once Richard was sentenced and carted off to his cell.

Nathan Leopold, Sr. had his own heart problems to deal with. He had a heart attack in 1929. During the time between the trial and his death, public ridicule and shame had forced him to move from his large home in Kenwood. Two of his other sons changed their names.

Clarence Darrow, meanwhile, had one more huge trial in him. This was the now-famous "Scopes Monkey Trial" where he defended a teacher accused of teaching evolution in school. His opponent during that trial was the equally famous William Jennings Bryant. That trial became a famous book, play, and movie entitled "Inherit the Wind."

As for the two young men? Well, they went off to spend their lives in prison, and things remained interesting for the two of them even despite this.

Chapter Thirteen
Leopold and Loeb in Prison

As the two young men heard the loud clanging door of Joliet prison close behind them, prison officials, at first, made sure that the two men would stay apart. It was widely believed, in fact it had been argued in their defense, that the two of them together made a very dangerous combination. As it was, Joliet Penitentiary was a dangerous place in those days and it was felt that the two of them together would only add to that danger.

This plan didn't last however. The two young men seemed destined to end up getting together, working together, and becoming completely linked. After only a year behind bars, though, the two young men were nothing like the cocky, arrogant, media-loving showboats that they had been during their trial. They were cautious, unwilling to talk to reporters.

"I can't talk to you," said Loeb, "I'd like to say something, but I'm afraid I'll get in bad."

In 1932, the two of them teamed up to try to improve the lives of their fellow prisoners. They opened a school along with other inmates of some education. Leopold and Loeb became the school administrators and they also taught classes.

It wasn't something that would last, however. Prison is not a fun place no matter how famous you may have become. So, the mastermind behind the crime, or so it is believed, Richard Loeb was attacked by his cellmate.

It was January 28, 1936, and James E. Day attacked Loeb while they were in the shower with a straight razor. Before he could be stopped, he had slashed Loeb over fifty times and the young man was bleeding to death. He was rushed into surgery and seven different surgeons worked on him at once, but it was too late, and Loeb had lost too much blood. He was thirty-two years old and he was gone. Strangely, it was his friend Nathan Leopold who was charged with washing the blood from his friend's body.

Leopold wrote about it years later when he wrote a book about his life and said,

"We covered him at last with a sheet, but after a moment, I folded the sheet back from his face and sat down on a stool by the table where he lay. I wanted a long last look at him. For, strange as it may sound, he had been by best pal.

"In one sense, he was also the greatest enemy I have ever had. For my friendship with him had cost me—my life. It was he who had originated the idea of committing the crime, he who planned it, he who largely carried it out. It was he who had insisted on doing what we eventually did. Dick was a living contradiction.

"As I sat now by his cooling, bleeding corpse, the strangeness of that contradiction, that basic, fundamental ambivalence of his character, was born in on me.

"For Dick possessed more of the truly fine qualities than almost anyone else I have ever known. Not just the superficial social grace. Those, of course, he possessed to the *nth* degree. But the more fundamental, more important qualities of character, too, he possess in full measure. He was loyal to a fault. He could be sincere; he could be honestly and selflessly dedicated. His devotion to the school proves that. He truly, deeply wanted to help his fellow man.

"How, I mused, could these personality traits coexist with the other side of Dick's character? It didn't make sense! For there was another side. Dick just didn't have the faintest trace of conventional morality. Not just before our incarceration. Afterward, too. I don't believe he ever, to the day of his death, felt truly remorseful for what he had done. Sorry that we had been caught, of course, but remorse for the murder itself? I honestly don't think so."

As for Day, the man who had shared a cell with Loeb and then killed him, he claimed Loeb had made sexual advances toward him. This didn't really explain how Day had gotten behind Loeb and slashed him from behind. The prison officials stated that Loeb and Day had argued many times—usually related to money. Day attempted to plead that he was acting in self-defense even though he was untouched and unharmed. Despite all of this, he was found not guilty.

As far as Nathan Leopold, he devoted himself to learning and being as quiet as possible while in prison. He was already a hugely intelligent man who spoke fifteen languages. While in prison, he learned twelve more while also studying math and other subjects. He worked in the prison library and continued to help run the prison school. In what spare time he still had, he raised canaries and worked on a malaria project.

Leopold spent years shunning the press and living quietly in his cell. Eventually, however, once the 1950s arrived, he would try to rehabilitate the image the public had of him. He started talking to the press, telling his story and that of Richard Loeb. After a time, the positive PR began to work and he got a parole hearing. At the time, the State's Attorney, a man named John Gutknecht, was opposed to Leopold ever getting out and vigorously and publicly opposed his release.

For that first hearing, Nathan Leopold was turned down in his bid to earn his freedom. The Parole Board decided to wait twelve years before listening to another possible parole possibility for Leopold, and this was the longest continuance in the history of Illinois at the time.

Despite this, March of 1958 came and Nathan Leopold was released from prison. He had served thirty-three years behind bars. As soon as he was released, Leopold moved to Puerto Rico in order to avoid any publicity—or press or harassment—by the public.

Leopold continued to study and even wrote a book about birds in Puerto Rico. He also got a Masters Degree from the University of Puerto Rico and found steady work.

Eventually, Leopold married a woman named Trudi Feldman Garcia de Quevada. They lived quietly together for ten years and then Nathan Leopold died quietly of a heart attack at the age of sixty-six.

With that, the Trial of the Century finally came to an end. In the subsequent years many have forgotten this case, except for those familiar with Hitchcock or the movie *Compulsion* starring Orson Welles. Some of the names are famous, such as Clarence Darrow, but the case itself seems murky all of these years later.

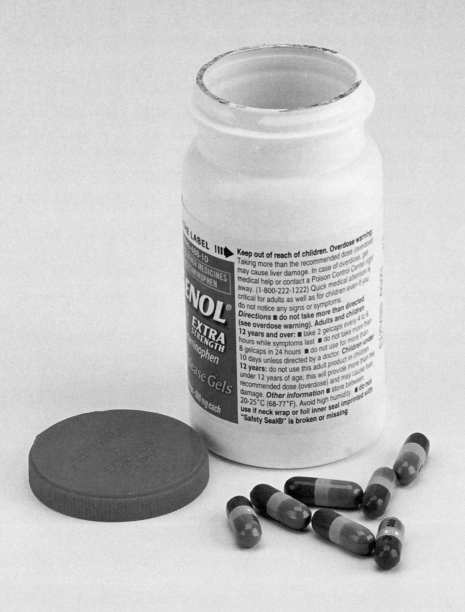

Keep out of reach of children. Overdose warning.
Taking more than the recommended dose (overdose)
may cause liver damage. In case of overdose, get
medical help or contact a Poison Control Center right
away. (1-800-222-1222) Quick medical attention is
critical for adults as well as for children even if you
do not notice any signs or symptoms.
Directions ■ do not take more than directed
(see overdose warning). **Adults and children
12 years and over:** ■ take 2 gelcaps every 4 to 6
hours while symptoms last ■ do not take more than
8 gelcaps in 24 hours ■ do not use for more than
10 days unless directed by a doctor. **Children under
12 years:** do not use this adult product in children
under 12 years of age; this will provide more than the
recommended dose (overdose) and may cause liver
damage. **Other information** ■ store between
20-25°C (68-77°F). Avoid high humidity. ■ do not
use if neck wrap or foil inner seal imprinted with
"Safety Seal®" is broken or missing

An Introduction
Take Two "Aspirin" and Call Me In The Morning...

In 1982, the city of Chicago was once again on the front page of every newspaper and the lead story on every newscast. This time, however, the implications would have far-reaching effects into nearly every corner of modern life. At the same time, the crime would nearly bring a multi-billion dollar company to its knees.

Johnson and Johnson is and was a major corporation providing products of all kinds. One of the biggest products that they still produce to this day is Tylenol Extra Strength. Normally, this is a product taken by people in pain or suffering from fevers to relieve their symptoms. It would not be too far out of place to say that the Tylenol name and even Johnson and Johnson were some of the most trusted names on the consumer market.

All of that changed in September of 1982, when several shocking deaths were attributed to people taking tainted Tylenol capsules. It stabbed at the heart of people everywhere. It was entirely random, but centered on the western suburbs of Chicago. While it may not have killed the rich and famous, it altered the way the world would package food, medicine, and consumable products from that time forward.

The company faced financial ruin. The entire country was in a panic. The city of Chicago actually advocated for the canceling of trick or treating that Halloween. It launched a massive manhunt.

Of course, as you may know, the man or men responsible for this act of consumer terrorism were never caught. The case, to this day, remains open.

Chapter Fourteen
Feeling Sick

The crime that would stun the world began on September 29, 1982, in Elk Grove Village, Illinois, a suburb of Chicago, located just west of O'Hare Airport. It was just before dawn, still dark, the sun still a few hours away in the Kellerman household. Mary Kellerman awoke to find her throat sore and her nose runny. She felt sick and she walked into her parents' room to tell them she wasn't feeling well. Her parents awoke, felt her forehead, and then went off to give her something for her fever. She was given one Extra-Strength Tylenol capsule. Mary and her parents returned to their respective beds and went back to sleep. At seven a.m., Mary's parents awoke again. Mary's mother went in to see how she was feeling and found her on the floor of the bathroom. The frantic mother called the paramedics and Mary was rushed to the hospital.

Although the doctors worked furiously on her, it was no use. She was pronounced dead and the doctors originally thought her death might have been because of a stroke or something natural. No one had any reason to suspect foul play at this point.

Things were about to get much worse that day for anyone wanting some relief for their pain. Later that same, day a man named Adam Janus called the paramedics. Janus was a resident of another Chicago suburb called Arlington Heights. He was in great distress, and by the time the paramedics arrived, he too was collapsed on the floor with his breathing labored and his blood pressure life-threateningly low. Janus was rushed to the hospital and the doctors worked on him feverishly. Again, though, it was to no avail.

His pupils were fixed and dilated. He was pronounced dead shortly after arriving in the ER. Given his symptoms and still with no idea about tainted capsules, the doctors theorized he must have died from a heart attack. Sadly, the tragedy of the Janus family was only beginning.

That evening, the Janus' family gathered at his home to discuss funeral arrangements. Janus's brother and his brother's new bride both complained of having headaches. The stress of having lost a family member appeared to be too much for them.

Janus' brother wandered into the kitchen where he found a bottle of Extra-Strength Tylenol. He took one of the capsules and gave one to his wife. In mere minutes, both the wife and brother were on the floor. The other family members called an ambulance and they were both rushed to the hospital.

Janus' brother was declared dead minutes after entering the hospital. His wife held on for a while, but died two days later. This time people got suspicious. At first, theories abounded that gas may be leaking somewhere within the Janus home. A Dr. Kim at Northwest Community Hospital, where all three family members had been taken, consulted with a John B. Sullivan at the Rocky Mountain Poison Center to discuss the effects of poison gases. As the two men discussed the case, Sullivan stated the symptoms sounded more like cyanide poisoning than anything else. Kim ordered blood samples taken from the deceased and sent them to the lab for testing. As Dr. Kim was waiting for the results of his lab tests, two firemen were discussing the strange cases that they had heard about in the area of people suddenly dropping dead on the floor. Of particular interest was the Janus family.

One firefighter, Phillip Cappitelli, from the Arlington Heights Fire Department, was discussing the Janus case with a friend, Richard Keyworth, from the Elk Grove Village Fire Department. Keyworth was familiar with the Kellerman incident and mentioned that Mary Kellerman's parents had informed the paramedics that she had complained of cold symptoms but had only taken some Extra-Strength Tylenol. Cappitelli made a phone call to the paramedics who had taken the Janus' to the hospital and asked if Extra-Strength Tylenol had been found on the premises there as well. The two firemen were surprised to find that it had.

The next call was to the police department. The bottles at both the Kellerman and Janus homes were taken by the police for testing. The next morning, both the labs from Dr. Kim and the tests on the capsules taken by police were confirmed. The Cook County chief toxicologist, Michael Shaffer, had discovered that each bottle contained capsules that had been emptied and refilled with about 65 milligrams of cyanide.

The blood tests backed this up by confirming the victims' blood was filled with deadly cyanide. Johnson and Johnson, the parent company of McNeil Consumer Products, the makers of Extra-Strength Tylenol, were contacted. A massive recall of product was ordered, almost immediately, by the company. Warnings were also sent to doctors, hospitals, and wholesalers of the potential danger with the product. This did not stop people who had already purchased tainted bottles, however. Mary Reiner was twenty-seven years old and lived in Winfield, Illinois, another suburb of Chicago. She had just given birth to her son and was still recovering. She took some Extra-Strength Tylenol to help with the pain. She was dead a few hours later. Paula Prince, a thirty-five-year-old flight attendant with United Airlines was found dead in her apartment. The police found tainted capsules. The seventh victim was thirty-five-year-old Mary McFarland of Elmhurst. The news story hit the national news shortly after McFarland died. The city of Chicago went into a panic. The entire country also panicked. In order to stop citizens from taking Tylenol, the suburban police drove through the Chicago area using loudspeakers to warn them of taking Tylenol products. The public began throwing out their bottles of Tylenol regardless of the actual brand. Area hospitals were flooded with phone calls. People became convinced that every ache and pain was somehow connected to cyanide poisoning. The head of the Seattle Poison Control Center made a statement informing the public that, had they actually been victims of cyanide poisoning, the poison would act so fast they would be unlikely to even be able to reach the phone to call anyone. Many states throughout the country banned outright the sale of any Tylenol products until further notice. Retailers across the country began removing Tylenol from their shelves and disposing of them and refused to put any more on the shelves until answers came. The serial numbers of the bottles that had been found in the victim's homes were released. The FDA stated that it appeared only products containing that lot number was of any real concern. However, most stores, due to concern from the public, still decided to remove all Tylenol products.

Johnson and Johnson issued statements confirming the recall which ended up costing the company $125 million. They also set up a nationwide hotline for people to receive current information and find out about safety measures. They announced that the facilities where the poisoned lots had been made were being checked to see if someone had accidentally placed the poison into the product at production. It was ultimately determined that this was not the case. This meant the poisonings were not an accident. The FBI, FDA, and local law enforcement agencies joined forces and established task forces to try to track down the person who had deliberately tainted the pills.

Chapter Fifteen
The Investigation

The problem for investigators was that there was no evidence. There were no witnesses. The bottles belonging to the victims had been handled by too many people to provide prints. There was also still the fear of tainted bottles still being in the public domain.

The law enforcement agencies set up hotlines to collect tips. The hotlines and task forces were flooded with calls from people concerned that medication they had in their homes was tainted. Also, of course, there was nothing stopping the "Tylenol Terrorist" from tainting more products if he so desired. In early October 1982, another tainted bottle was discovered by police as they checked bottles removed from local shelves. Johnson and Johnson issued a $1,000 reward for information leading to the apprehension of the criminal who had done this. Authorities had no way of knowing how many other bottles were tampered with and they were worried that the terrorist may have tampered with products beyond Tylenol. Six Chicago-based stores were discovered having products that contained the tampered capsules. The Jewel Foods store in Arlington Heights, the Jewel Foods in Grove Village, Walgreens in Chicago, and Frank's Finer Foods in Winfield were the outlets named as having the tainted bottles on their shelves. Each store was found to have at least one tampered bottle, and within that bottle, were three to ten tampered capsules. The one exception was an Osco Drug that had two bottles found to contain cyanide-laced capsules. Authorities struggled to find patterns within this crime. Some believed that the placements were entirely random. Still other officials believed that the locations were in a pattern meant to be discovered. Some theorized that the perpetrator had a grudge against one or more of the store chains. Some thought he might have a grudge against Johnson and Johnson. Some felt that maybe he lived near or within a short distance of the semi-circle of stores where tainted bottles were found.

More clues began to emerge. Tests revealed that the exact poison used was potassium-cyanide. This type of poison was available to those who worked in industries like gold and silver mining, fertilizer production, steel plating, film processing, and chemical manufacturing. This brought up the theory that the terrorist may be working within one of those industries. About a month after the first killings, the investigators took someone into custody. He was a forty-eight-year-old dockhand and amateur chemist. He worked for a company that supplied Tylenol to at least two of the stores where tainted bottles had been found. Under questioning, the suspect admitted to having access to cyanide. Investigators also revealed that a search of his apartment found weapons of all sizes and shapes, two one-way tickets to Thailand, and a book that had instructions on how to stuff poison in to capsules as a method for murder. Despite this evidence, there was nothing to specifically link him to any of the tainted bottles. Lacking this connection, they could not charge him with murder in any of the deaths due to poisoning. He was charged with illegal possession of firearms and eventually released on bond. No sooner did this suspect vanish back into the distance than a new suspect suddenly emerged. Johnson and Johnson received a handwritten letter demanding $1 million for the end of the poisonings. The letter writer demanded that the company respond to his demands by putting some kind of ad or article in the *Chicago Tribune*. The corporation went to the authorities instead. The authorities were able to trace the letters to a man named James W. Lewis.

Lewis seemed to fit the profile. He was a known con artist and was wanted in connection with a murder and jewel robbery in Kansas City. A warrant was immediately issued for his arrest. The FBI and Illinois Law Enforcement agencies began tracing the last known locations of Lewis and his wife, LeAnn. This chase led them across Illinois, Missouri, Kansas, and Texas. The agencies began plastering posters and pictures of the couple all over the country. Meanwhile tests continued on the bottles taken off of store shelved in the Chicago area. One bottle was found to contain poison and was found in a store very close to where Paula Prince had purchased her bottle of tainted pills. This bottle was checked for fingerprints and other hair and fiber clues. They came up empty.

A letter arrived in the offices of the *Chicago Tribune* from someone named Robert Richardson stating that he and his wife had nothing to do with the poisonings. Robert Richardson was a known alias of Lewis. This letter was traced to New York City. The search for Lewis began to concentrate there. Libraries and police stations were notified and sent pictures of the two suspects. Johnson and Johnson, by November, announced that they would be re-introducing the products that had been recalled to the market. They announced that the products would now be packaged in new tamper-resistant, triple-sealed packaging. They also announced they would release $2.50 coupon towards the purchase of any Tylenol product. The business world held its breath and wondered whether or not consumer confidence would be restored or if one of the largest corporations in the world would suffer financial collapse. To everyone's surprise consumer confidence was restored. In less than two months, the company had regained ninety-eight percent of the market share they had lost due to the murders. The FBI received a tip from a librarian in New York, who said she recognized Lewis from the pictures that had been sent of Lewis and his wife. The FBI and surrounded the reading room of the New York Public Library. Lewis was arrested without a struggle and underwent questioning. The following week his spouse, LeAnn Lewis, turned herself in to Chicago police. Despite handwriting analysis that seemed to show the extortion letters were written by Lewis, he and his wife denied having anything to do with the letters or the poisonings. An article in *Newsweek* then stated a second extortion letter was found at the White House telling the President that a bomb would be placed at the White House and more poisonings would occur unless President Reagan changed his tax policies. Lewis also denied writing this letter, even though there was evidence to suggest he had.

Beyond the letters, law enforcement could not find any other evidence to connect the Lewises to the Tylenol poisonings. Further investigations showed that the Lewises were staying in a hotel in New York when the bottles would have been tampered with. Further investigations showed LeAnn Lewis had been at her regular job in New York during the time when the poisoner would have been tampering with and placing the tampered bottles in the Chicago area. The law enforcement officials also could not find any evidence that the Lewises had been in Chicago at any time during the poisonings. The Lewises were ultimately charged and found guilty of extortion and credit card fraud and were sentenced to twenty years in prison.

The FBI was forced to admit that the Tylenol Terrorist was still on the loose.

Chapter Sixteen
The FBI Profile

At the time of the killings, the idea of profiling a suspect was not entirely new. In fact, profiling was essentially what the alienists had done going all the way back to the Leopold and Loeb case. However, releasing the profile to the public was something relatively new.

The FBI released what they believed was an accurate profile of the killer. The Tylenol Terrorist was probably male and a loner. It was also believed that he was likely to have received treatment for some kind of extreme mental disorder like depression or anger-control problems. He may have spent time complaining about society or feelings of wrongdoings committed by society against him. He may have even reached out to people of power or influence to express his feelings of injustice and perhaps felt that he was not taken seriously—which only fueled his anger toward society. He was also likely to be living in and around the Chicago area. He probably owned a car or truck, due to the distances between the stores where the poisoned capsules were found. The capsules were not very well hidden. Most of the capsules with poison bulged or were deformed. However, the victims simply never noticed. It was suggested that the killer was rather incompetent, but had feelings of superiority. He was probably not particularly intelligent. Also, the killer may have worked in a profession that had easy access to cyanide. Finally, it was suggested the killer had a menial job with very low wages. Whether or not this profile is of any help is something still open to debate.

Even at the time of the crimes, the profile was criticized,

and has continued to be, over the years. Critics state that it is too general and provides nothing that could be of any use to the investigators. However, some others have argued that the profile provides some valuable insight into the potential living habits of the terrorist.

Since no one has ever been brought to justice for this crime, it remains to be seen how close to the truth the profile may have come.

Chapter Seventeen
The Copycats

While the search continued for the man who poisoned capsules in Chicago, a couple of notorious copycats emerged and continued to foster the fear throughout the nation. Congress passed a law that made product tampering a federal offense. The FDA created requirements for over-the-counter medications and required that they be made tamper-resistant. Law enforcement agencies across the country were flooded with reports of products been tampered with.

In 1986, a woman by the name of Stella Nickell was arrested and convicted of killing her spouse using poisoned Excedrin tablets. She had grown bored with their relationship and had taken out huge insurance policies on him. If she was able to prove that his death was unnatural, she stood to gain even greater amounts of money. Nickel evidently tried to make it look like he had been a victim of a random poisoner, and not only tampered with medication her spouse took, but put tampered pills in several stores. A woman by the name of Sue Snow died from taking tampered pills. Nickell was convicted and sentenced to ninety years in prison. In 1991, another tampering scheme was discovered. This time it was tainted Sudafed. A man named Joseph Meling was convicted of attempting to kill his wife with the tampered tablets. Once again, Meling had taken out a large policy on his wife and had attempted to make her death look like part of random poisonings. At least two people died from taking tampered tablets while Meling's wife actually survived the attempt on her life. As for the person who murdered seven people in the Chicago area, no suspect has ever been caught and charged. The reward offered by Johnson and Johnson is still unclaimed. All leads have long since grown cold and no further evidence has ever been produced. However, as advances in crime detection occur, there is always the chance some new evidence can be found or perhaps that someone may come forward who knows something. After all, it took years before a relative of the Unabomber came forward to identify him. While the murders remain unsolved, the impact of the murders continues to this day. The way in which food and medication is packaged changed after this incident. Anyone who has ever struggled with the plastic seal around a bottle of aspirin has experienced, first-hand, the radical changes that were instituted in packaging the foods and medicine we take to this day.

Chapter Eighteen
The Company

Luckily for Johnson and Johnson, the public was forgiving. The company did everything it could to earn back the trust of the public and they were largely successful. In fact, consumer studies at the time showed that in as little as six months after the poisonings, the public's trust in the company had returned.

The makers of Tylenol testified before Congress. They revealed the new tamper-proof bottles that they hoped would prevent further incidents such as these. They also took out television and print ads where they offered coupons and discounts to people to try Tylenol again. They touted their new safety bottles. Whatever it was, perhaps the earnest nature of the ads, it seemed to bring people back to the product.

Needless to say, other companies were forced to follow suit. Everything from medicine to toothpaste and pre-packaged food items were suddenly redesigned to make them tamper-proof. Of course, the copycat crimes show that doing this completely is impossible.

When the first murders happened, many sounded the death knell for Johnson and Johnson. By acting quickly and by being honest with the public, the multi-billion dollar corporation was able to turn the public outcries to their favor and save themselves from bankruptcy court.

Conclusion
A City of Crime?

So, with all of the notorious crimes and murders brought about by people of wealth in and around the Chicago area, does this mean that Chicago itself is a city built on crime? Is Chicago, in fact, a worse crime area than other cities?

Statistics certainly say differently. Sure, Chicago has crime, and some of it has become world-famous, but it is hardly a match for the crimes of the celebrities in Los Angeles, or the sheer number of crimes you find in News York.

The one thing that seems to set Chicago apart is the sheer brutality of the crimes themselves. It wasn't enough just to kidnap for the sake of ransom, for example, but Leopold and Loeb had to brutally murder their young captive just for the sheer thrill. It wasn't enough for Silas Jayne to bilk old women and other people out of money for horses that weren't worth a dime, but he had to kill anyone and everyone who got in his way, including his own brother.

Of course, the crimes and murders continue. Chicago, for example, was a stop along the way for serial killer Andrew Cunanan. He killed millionaire building designer Lee Miglin here in Chicago before heading to Florida to kill fashion designer Gianni Versace and then himself. Chicago was also the location of the notorious "Brown's Chicken" massacre in the 90s and the murders of shoppers and workers at a Lane Bryant store.

Chicago is a city that works hard and plays hard. It has a reputation of being a tough city. The brutal winters followed by intense summers have helped make the Chicago residents a very hearty and very intense lot. They are also fiercely protective of Chicago and its image.

At the same time, there is a strange kind of pride Chicagoans feel about some of their most notorious citizens. No one would dispute that Al Capone was a brutal killer, but he is also looked upon by many in Chicago with a kind of pride.

Will Chicago every fully shed its image as a city for murderers and criminals? It's trying to, but it may be impossible to do when you have a rogues' gallery containing names like Capone, Gacy, and Speck. Of course, there are still crimes being committed here to this day. What does the future hold? It's hard to say, of course, but if it's strange, a bit odd, or just a bit different than anything else you hear of anywhere else, you can probably bet it happened here in Chicago.

Bibliography

ABC7 News Chicago. "ABC 7 I-Team learns identities of people reportedly behind Helen Brach's Murder." http://abclocal.go.com/wls/

Beck, Melinda and Agrest, Susan (February 24, 1986). "Again, a Tylenol Killer." *Newsweek*. National Affaires, page 25. United States Edition.

Beck, Melinda and Foote, Donna (November 8, 1982). "The Tylenol Letter." *Newsweek*. National Affaires, page 32. United States Edition.

Beck, Melinda; Monroe, Sylvester; Buckley, Jerry (October 25, 1982). "Tylenol: Many Leads, No Arrests." *Newsweek*. National Affaires, page 30. United States edition.

Beck, Melinda; Monroe, Sylvester; Prout, Linda; Hager, Mary; LaBreque, Ron (October 11, 1982). "The Tylenol Scare." *Newsweek*. National Affaires, page 32. United States edition.

Douglas, John and Olshaker, M. (1997). *Journey into Darkness*. Mass Market Paperback.

Ghost Guides: The Dark Side of Chicago. www.ghostguides.com

Higdon, Hal, *Crime of the Century: The Leopold & Loeb Case* (G. P. Putnam's Sons, 1975).

Hobbs, Dawn. Ask John Douglas, who wrote the book on how to profile killers."

Kowalski, Wally. "The Tylenol Murders."

Leopold, Nathan F., Jr., *Life Plus 99 Years*. Doubleday, 1958

Manning, Jason (2000). The Tylenol Murders."

McKernan, Maureen, *The Amazing Crime and Trial of Leopold and Loeb*. New American Library, 1957.

Newsweek (December 27, 1982). "A Librarian Ends A Tylenol Manhunt." National Affaires, page 19. United States Edition.

O'Shea, Gene. "Blood Feud." http://www.ipsn.org/news/blood_feud_by_gene_oshea.htm (this was also the basis for the chapter about Silas murdering his brother)

Stravinsky, John, (June 2002). "Silas Jayne: Horse Breeder/Show Jumper." *Chicago* Magazine.

Tierney, Kevin, *Classics of the Courtroom*, Volume VIII, "Clarence Darrow's Sentencing Speech in *State of Illinois v. Leopold and Loeb*.

Tierney, Kevin, *Darrow: A Biography* (Thomas Y. Crowell, 1979) and

Tifft, Susan (October 11, 1982). "Poison Madness in the Midwest." *Time*.

Weird & Haunted Chicago. www.prairieghosts.com

Wikipedia. www.wikipedia.org.